T0065270

SIERRA LEONE PRIVATE INVESTMENT AND FINANCIAL SECTOR DEVELOPMENT

TRENDS AND STATISTICS

DR. EZEKIEL K. DURAMANY-LAKKOH

SIERRA LEONE PRIVATE INVESTMENT AND FINANCIAL SECTOR DEVELOPMENT
TRENDS AND STATISTICS

iUniverse books may be ordered through booksellers or by contacting:

iUniverse
1663 Liberty Drive
Bloomington, IN 47403
www.iuniverse.com
844-349-9409

ISBN: 978-1-6632-0100-3 (sc)
ISBN: 978-1-6632-0101-0 (e)

Library of Congress Control Number: 2020921325

Print information available on the last page.

iUniverse rev. date: 11/28/2020

ACKNOWLEDGEMENTS

This book and I have greatly benefited from lively, inspiring discussions with academics, friends, colleagues, and professionals in the areas of finance, economics, business, statistics, and politics. I would especially like to thank the almighty God for the strength and knowledge he accorded me in writing this book. My special thanks go to Dr Dante Bendu, dean of the faculty of social sciences and law, Fourah Bay College, for raising my interest in the area of accounting and finance, and Professor Joe A. D. Alie, dean of the school of postgraduate studies, University of Sierra Leone. Thanks to Professor John Mccpeak, deputy chair of the Department of Public Administration and International Relations, Maxwell School for Citizenship and Public Affairs, Syracuse University, for his inspiration in the field of economics. Thanks to Dr Komba D. Marah for his inspiration in financial economics, and to Professor E. K. Thompson for mentorship in the field of management and administration. Thanks to Dr Abdulai Sillah, deputy director of research at Bank of Sierra Leone, and Dr Bob Conteh, dean of postgraduate studies, University of Makeni, for their immense contribution in the field of econometrics and research, respectively.

Finally, I am grateful to the staff and faculty members of the Department of Accounting and Finance, Fourah Bay College (FBC) and the Institute of Public Administration and Management (IPAM) for their support throughout my years as a doctoral student.

CONTENTS

PART 1

Discussions and Descriptive
Statistical Analysis of Private
Investment in Sierra Leone

CHAPTER 1

Historical Economic Overview

The analysis in the book compares Sierra Leone with other African countries, especially Ghana. Sierra Leone shares similar socio-economic characteristics with other sub-Saharan African countries that were colonized mostly by the British and the French, gained independence around the same period, and have undertaken similar economic policy reforms after independence. Sierra Leone and Ghana have adopted similar fiscal policies for the past decades, guided by the World Bank, the International Monetary Fund (IMF), the African Development Bank (ADB), and the West Africa Monetary Agency (WAMA). The two countries have strong democracies and enjoy and suffer similar political instabilities, even though Sierra Leone suffered from a terrible eleven-year civil war. Sierra Leone and Ghana shared similar government policies in the past—for instance, subsidized petroleum product. Both countries have had fuel crises, both introduced a goods and services tax during the same period, and both restructured their national revenue collection systems.

Brief Overview of Sierra Leone

On 27 April 1961, Sierra Leone, a former British colony, gained independence from its former masters and established

1

a multiparty democracy. The country declared itself a republic in April 1971.

Information from World Guide (2015) indicates that the country is bordered on the north-east by Guinea, south-east by Liberia, and on the south-west by the Atlantic Ocean. The country has an area of 71,740 square kilometres (27,699 square miles), with an estimated population of more than seven million people in 2015. Geographical, political, and postcolonial struggles have posed huge economic challenges for the country over the years. After the declaration of independence in 1961, the country relied heavily on agriculture, trade, and mining for its economic growth. The main imports were food, medical supplies, and machinery from China, the United Kingdom, Germany, India, and the United States. Primary exports were diamonds, rutile, iron ore, and agricultural goods. Exports were mainly to China and Western countries. According to the *Sierra Rutile Handbook* (2000), in 1979, the country was identified as the world's largest producer of rutile, and in 1990 alone, total export of rutile amounted to 88,000 tons from which a revenue of USD 75 million was generated. Sierra Leone, like other Africa countries, has gone through a lot of political and civil conflicts. During 1967 and 1968, the country had three military coups, and until early 2000, political instability was a common issue that chased away investors. On 23 March 1991, rebels loyal to the Revolutionary United Front (RUF), supported by the then Liberia warlord Charles Taylor, attacked the country. This ended up in an eleven-year conflict that left more than fifty thousand men, women, and children dead, and the entire economy and revenue mobilization potential was decapitated. By the end of January 2002, Ahmed Tejan Kabba, the then president, declared the war over. Tens of thousands of combatants were disarmed, demobilized, and resettled into their communities. Some of these combatants played a very important role in the new Sierra Leone economy (Alie 2010).

After the end of the war, the economy of Sierra Leone was in very bad shape. During the eleven years, the tax administration structures were devastated. The government's ability to raise revenue was constrained by the attack and destruction of businesses all over the country. According to the Bureau of African Affairs at the US Department of States (2013), "Sierra Leone's brutal 1991–2002 Civil War destroyed infrastructures and truncated political, social, and economic development". The civil war hinders the ability of Sierra Leoneans to pay taxes because 75 per cent of the population was living under extreme poverty, and almost all the industries were shut down. Figure 1 shows the GDP growth rate. Figure 2 shows Sierra Leone's GDP per capita (PPP).

Sierra Leone's GDP Growth Rate, 2010–2019

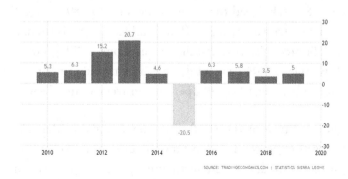

3

Sierra Leone's GDP Forecast

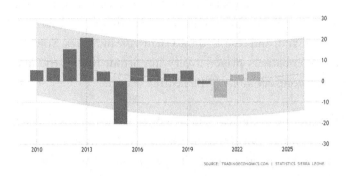

SOURCE: TRADINGECONOMICS.COM | STATISTICS SIERRA LEONE

Sierra Leone observed a steady GDP growth beginning in 2010, and 2013 was not only the biggest GDP growth for the country but also one of the largest growths in the world. This growth was triggered by the exploration of iron ore in the country. In mid-2014, the global price of iron ore fell by more than 80 per cent, bringing GDP from 20.7 in the previous year to only 4.6, and then there was a fall of 20.5 in 2015. Sierra Leone's PPP was approximately USD 750 at the start of the civil war. This fell to slightly above USD 600 in 2001, just before the end of the war. However, by the end of 2012, with the support of government revenue reforms, PPP was USD 1,400 and the country was ranked 189 amongst other countries in the region (like Zambia, Bennie, Tanzania, etc.). Sources also revealed that the economy's PPP grew on an average of 4.04 per cent during the war, and growth rate extended immensely to 89.2 per cent on average after the war.

The structure of the GDP after the war shows that the agriculture sector is important to revenue mobilization. The fall of the agriculture sector during the war precipitated the economic decline because more than 75 per cent of the population was employed in this sector (Sierra Leone PRSP 5, 87). Notwithstanding the collapse, then president of Sierra Leone, Dr Ahmed Tejan Kabba, declared in the Poverty Reduction Strategy Paper (2005) that "no Sierra Leonean will go to bed hungry by the year 2007". This declaration shifted the priority of government to agriculture, which boosted standard of living, encouraged industrialization, and increased the ability of citizens and corporate institutions to pay taxes. Figure 3 shows the percentage GDP contribution by sector in Sierra Leone.

Reforms have improved businesses and promoted growth in Sierra Leone. According to the African Economic Outlook (2009), in 2007 the GDP of Sierra Leone was driven mostly by agriculture, other services, and trade, with 58 per cent of the GDP coming from agriculture alone while trade and other services were contributing a total of 19.90 per cent and 10.4 per cent, respectively. The least came from electricity (9.5 per cent), which was supposed to be very important for industrial development.

The Organization for Economic Co-operation and Development's *African Outlook Report* (2011) detailed Sierra Leone's GDP base on purchasing power parity (PPP) valuation at USD 5.374 billion, with a per capita of USD 896 in 2011 and an annual real growth average of 6.4 per cent over the period 2003–2011. As reported in 2013, the reported growth jumped from 6.4 per cent in 2011 to 16.7 per cent in 2012. Most of the growth came from iron ore production, agriculture, services, and the boom in the construction industry. The country also reduced the current accounts deficit, as a percentage of GDP, from 52.3 per cent in 2011 to 44.0 per cent in 2012.

Sierra Leone, with the support of the international community, adopted several social and economic reform programs. Most of these reforms were on good governance and socio-economic growth. Apart from the MDGs which the government was implementing, the governments issued three important documents from 2005 to 2013.

i.   *The Poverty Reduction Strategy Paper 1* **(PRSP 1), 2005.** This was a joint IMF and Sierra Leone government initiative that outlined the strategic processes of economic recovery after the war. The PRSP outlined several macroeconomic, financial, and structural reforms; one of the reforms adopted was on "Domestic Revenue Mobilization".

ii. *The Poverty Reduction Strategy Paper 2* **(PRSP 2), 2008.** Following the PRSP 1, the PRSP 2, which is also called "the Agenda for Change", focuses on energy, agriculture, and transportation. To achieve these three priorities, the document noted "Fiscal Policy and Public Financial Management" as preconditions.

iii. *Agenda for Prosperity,* **2013.** This strategy focuses on roads and the enhancement of a secured middle class. In order to achieve these outcomes, the document emphasizes the importance to intensify "Domestic Revenue Mobilization".

Notwithstanding the economic challenges, the government of Sierra Leone opted to strengthen domestic revenue mobilization as a very important vehicle to transport economic growth. In an opening address to the Sierra Leone Parliament in 2013, the president of the Republic of Sierra Leone, Dr Ernest Bai Koroma, noted that

> As a result of our dedication to getting more from our own resources to fund the country's programs, NRA's revenue collection grown considerably to Le1.87 trillion in 2012. The NRA's contribution to Government expenditure has kept on increasing, reaching 70 per cent in 2012. In the first six months of the current year, domestic revenue contribution to government expenditure is slightly over 80 per cent. The NRA collected Le1.081 trillion against a target of Le1.042 trillion. We will stay focused on increasing revenues to fund our programs until we can fund 100 per cent of our development programs.

Meanwhile, GDP was expected to grow in 2016 and was expected to fall by 9 in 2020, according to statistics from Trading Economics (2019). From 2018 to 2020, GDP growth has been sluggish due to poor growth within the private sector. Government reforms of the private sector, especially the mining industry, are believed to be holding back growth. The government introduced several reforms within the mining industry, and some of these reforms saw the cancellation of licenses of even the largest mining companies in the country, resulting in 3.5 per cent GDP growth in 2018. Agriculture and service sectors were the main drivers of the 2019 economic growth.

Monetary Policy

Sierra Leone continued to conduct monetary policies using the indirect tools of monetary operations, mainly open-market operations, in 2008. The primary focus was the attainment of a single-digit inflation rate, even when the consequences of the United States recession had a negative impact on cost of production, which emanated from an increase in the import of petroleum commodities and foodstuff. The following was adopted to robustly contain inflationary pressure in the economy: Bank of Sierra Leone opted to eliminate the approval of parliament in making necessary and timely adjustments to the reserve's requirement of commercial banks. The objective was to eliminate the lag between the need for change in monetary policy in the circumstance when liquidity conditions may have changed. This bottleneck could render the reserve requirement ineffective as a monetary tool. Further to removing political bottleneck in the implementation of monetary policy, the bank placed strong requirements on foreign currency deposits and on domestic deposit, meeting the benchmark of both single currency and aggregate net open position at 15 per cent and 25 per cent, respectively.

The Agenda for Prosperity (2008) explained the plans to reduce the debt service burden of government in the short term by introducing long-term security with a minimum period of three to five years. This was directed towards institutions with long-term funds objectives. The introduction of policies to address effective secondary markets was all within the framework of the Sierra Leone government monetary policy.

Another area of concern was the replacement of a rediscount window in the secondary market with a fully operational interbank market and repurchase agreement (REPO). This is aimed at relating current window transactions to end-day liquidity requirements within the banking system.

The Central Bank of Sierra Leone believes that to obtain a clear line between securities for open market operations and those servicing the public sector borrowing requirement, there should be transparency in the open-market operations.

Debt Policy

The current focus of Sierra Leon debt policy is centred on improving the accuracy of information on debt data, which should be made available to all stakeholders within the debt management framework. The newly established Public Debt Unit and Budget Bureau, in collaboration with the Accountant General and the Central Bank, are now utilizing the Commonwealth Secretariat Debt Recording System to maintain data on debt with the sole aim of mitigating the risk of data inadequacies and accuracy.

The present debt-management strategy falls within three fundamental categories: external debt strategy, domestic debt strategy, and contingent liabilities strategy. As of June 2008, total public debt amounted to USD 580.1 million, whereas domestic debt was Le 1.2 trillion. External debt was 58 per cent of total public debt disclosure. However, as of 2013 domestic debt was more than 70 per cent of total debt.

The Ministry of Finance and Economic Development reported in 2012 that external debt policy geared towards avoiding a relapse into huge debt overload would constrain future economic development. Therefore, the Sierra Leone government made external debt management a key component in its agenda for prosperity. Under the HIPC initiative in 2006, the country benefited from debt cancellation worth about USD 904 million, as well as an MDRI debt cancellation of about USD 609.9 million from IMF and other countries.

In line with current initiative, the government, in collaboration with the World Bank, seeks to utilize the IDA debt reduction facility. The government conducted debt sustainability analysis to enable the analysis of long-term debt structures. The overall strategy included prioritizing grant finance over loans, especially for social sector investments; borrowing on concessional terms; prioritizing sectors to which loan reserves were to be directed; and strengthening legal framework and institutional capacity.

External and domestic debt management has been central to the Sierra Leone government's macroeconomic objectives. Debt, which includes short-term borrowing, such as government papers, domestic suppliers, contractors' arrears, and obtaining obligation bills, has been growing over the years. It was identified that the huge interest rate on such debt has outgrown government investment in all sectors. The main strategy in this area includes verifying domestic debt arrears within the medium-term expenditure framework to lengthen the maturity structure of government securities and to create cash flow relief on the budget, restricting central bank financing on the budget, and enhancing the liquidity forecasting framework.

The government has adopted a strong stance on MDAs from taking financial obligations which have resulted in huge contingent liabilities in the budget.

CHAPTER 2

Fiscal Policy and Private Investment in Sierra Leone

Applications of Fiscal Policy in Sierra Leone

Sierra Leone was negatively affected by double shocks: the plunge of global iron ore prices and the outbreak of the deadly Ebola virus in 2014. During this period, the government mobilized about Le 3.2 trillion from fiscal revenue and grants, and this accounted for a 0.9 per cent fall from the previous period.

The Ministry of Finance and Economic Development (2014) stated that due to the Ebola virus outbreak of 2014, government expenditures increased by 59 per cent from 2013, the biggest of the budgetary deficits. During the same period, there was an increase in total expenditure and lending by 1 per cent (of GDP). That was, however, less than the predetermined number for the previous year.

Apart from the falling prices of iron ore (one of the country's main exports) in the world market, the lion's share of Sierra Leone's 2014 budget was allocated to the Health Ministry, thus causing reduced expenditures on other infrastructural developments, such as roads, government business enterprises, schools, and more.

The National Revenue Authority in 2014 adjusted the country's income tax rates for both individuals and corporations at 30 per cent, and in early 2016, personal income taxes was increased to 35 per cent. Individual income tax rates range from the least taxable income of 15 per cent (Le 300,000) to the highest rate of 35 per cent (Le 750,000 and above). There is no capital gains tax on both residential and nonresidential personal incomes. The 2009 Goods and Services Act combined seven previously different taxes (import sales tax, domestic sales tax, entertainment tax, restaurant and food tax, messages tax, hotel accommodation tax, and professional services tax) and brought the goods and services tax (GST) with a tax rate of 15 per cent for taxable supplies of Le 200 million.

Since then, the country has been recovering from so many challenges ranging from poverty to diseases, high rates of illiteracy, and unemployment. In 2014, the deadly Ebola virus struck the country, hampering almost all the economic activities within Sierra Leone. In 2013, the United States embassy in Freetown published an economic document titled "Investment Climate Statement", from which an analysis of key investment-related topics about Sierra Leone were presented in relation to the Sierra Leone economy. The document covered issues such as the country's openness to and restriction upon foreign investment, transparency of the regulatory systems, right to private ownership and establishment, efficient capital market and portfolio investment, and competition from state-owned enterprises.

On the foreign direct investment analysis, it is evident that in terms of infrastructural projects, the Chinese are the dominant contractors. The China Railway Seventh Group Corporation is constructing the biggest road project in the country. Other Chinese companies were in contract with the government of Sierra Leone for the construction of railways, repairs of airports, building hospitals, and other private investments in the mining, fishing, and tourism sectors.

According to the investment code of 2005, which is the guidance code against foreign investor limits, discrimination or denial of treatment is in effect and optimally obeyed. The only restriction on foreign investment is on the mining sector. The restriction requires that any investment in mining of an amount that is less than USD 500,000 must be owned by a Sierra Leonean at a minimum of 25 per cent holdings (i.e. a maximum of 75 per cent foreign ownership of the total investment). It is enforced to protect local artisan miners.

The country has an open trade policy, with almost all nontariff barriers being removed. Tariff rates are of the same standards as the rest of the other ECOWAS countries, with little exportation and importation licenses required (applicable to a few types of products).

The judicial system is considered inefficient, corrupt, and slow in passing judgements. Many international bodies were trying to undertake projects that would enhance the judiciary's efficiency in executing contract laws.

The level of transparency of the regulatory systems is associated with inefficient enforcement and excessive court delays. There is a government-consolidated establishment named One Stop Centre which enables investors to access and register all the necessary licenses and permits in a single department. Regulatory procedures are perceived to be highly exposed to corruption. Some of the problems faced by investors include high tax rates, licenses, and contract enforcement. There are equal opportunities for both local and foreign investments; the regulators don't have any discriminatory forces against foreign investors.

On the right to privately establish and own businesses, Sierra Leone allows both domestic and foreign investors to start business enterprises and operate them according to the country's investment policies. The investment climate also allows investors to freely acquire available businesses and dispose their holdings from other entities, or to sell their entire business enterprise to readily interested prospective buyers according to law.

Issues relating to the idea of capital markets and portfolio investment, as well as access to credit facilities, are difficult to obtain from the private sector (i.e. commercial banks) because land tenure systems make it difficult for investors to produce collateral. Foreign investors are allowed to own land in Sierra Leone, and it is legal for foreigners to lease from either the government or citizens. The use of bank overdraft remains the most common way private entities maintain credit. Portfolio investing is not popular in the Sierra Leone economy because the country is dominated by cash-driven exchanges with fewer electronic transactions. The 2007 established stock exchange hasn't attracted many investors and remains relatively small, with only one traded stock available to date.

Interest rates can be as high as 25 per cent and as low as 14 per cent depending on the customer's banking relationship and history in relation to the amount of financial transactions. However, interest rates are reducing as the number of competing commercial banks is on the increase.

Private entities are normally faced with competition from state-owned enterprises. According to Sierra Leone's investment policies, whenever government business enterprises (GBEs) and privately owned entities are in competition, the same terms and conditions are applied to both enterprises. The equity is applicable to credit facilities, markets, and all other business-enhancing operations. Communications, transport, and energy are the sectors most likely to experience competition between public and private institutions within the economy. One of the most critical advantages that state-owned enterprises have over private entities is their reporting obligations; only private entities are required by law to publish their financial statements, which must be audited by a reputable private audit firm. Government business enterprises are required to submit their financial reports to state supervisory committees.

There is a high expectation of corporate social responsibilities from businesses operating in Sierra Leone because the government, civil society, and NGO normally intensify the need for businesses to give back to society. Sectors such as mining and telecommunications are in high demand, and their CSR is geared towards programmes such as education, health, and sometimes the social sector (sport and entertainment).

The country's labour laws encourage employees in the formal sector to form unions, with the exception of the military, police, and other government forces. The rights of labour unions in the private sector are protected by law. The industries most influenced by labour unionism are mining, agriculture, and health. Labour unions can organize protests with the condition of noticing the police government after twenty-one days. Sierra Leone's labour laws, however, prohibit compulsory and child labour. The law allows children to participate in labour-related activities as follows: children aged 13 years can participate in light work, aged 15 can work full-time, and aged 18 can do hazardous work. The average work hours per week is set at forty; anything above that must be added to the employee's earnings as 50 per cent overtime. Employees can be dismissed with or without compensation depending on the gravity of the cause; in extreme circumstances, workers' contracts can be terminated without compensation if they have been warned twice.

Private Investment

Private investment represents the total value of machinery, plants, and buildings acquired by firms for the purpose of production or capital accumulation. Private investment is the independent variable in this investigation.

The private investment curve in the following figure shows the trend of private investment in Sierra Leone from 1980 to 2015. The figure shows a series of rises and falls in the private investment curve, with a big step between 1990 and 1992 and between 1996 and 1997. Between 1997 and 2001, private investment falls to a negative. This was during the civil war, when Sierra Leone's manufacturing, agricultural, and services sectors were hardly functioning.

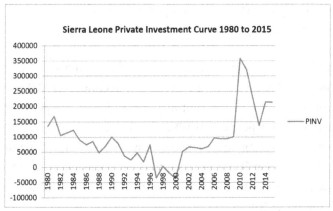

Source: (Constructed from the study data)

After the decline, private investment rose by 311 per cent from 1995 to 1996; this was a result of the confidence investors had in the economy after the return to democratic rule and the first multiparty elections. After the year 2000, private investment rose exponentially, with a big rise in 2009. Private investment rose again from 8 per cent in 2009 to 254 per cent in 2010 during the commencement of African Minerals operations. The sharp rise was accorded to the investment in the mining industry, especially the iron ore sector.

Private investment played a significant role in the economic development of Sierra Leone, especially in the years after 2009. This included an increase in demand for capital goods, which in turn increased domestic expenditure and enlarged production base. The boom in private investments, as a result of the mining industry, improved the foreign exchange in the economy until 2014, when there was a fall in the global price of iron ore. The fall in prices affected some of the biggest companies in Sierra Leone and even caused the closure of two of the largest mining companies, African Minerals and London Mining.

In Ghana, private investment has been fluctuating, especially since the 1980s, because there was a decline from 8.0 per cent in 1975 to 2.9 per cent in 1983, and from 4.4 per cent in 1984 to 2.5 per cent in 1992. There was in improvement in private investment in Ghana from 2.5 per cent in 1992 to 12.7 per cent in 2000, and then from 16.7 per cent in 2001 to 17.0 per cent in 2005. A 6 per cent decline was subsequently observed in 2013.

In 1990, Chhibber and Mansoor had related private investment challenges in Ghana to both internal and external economic shocks. During the 1980s, Sierra Leone and Ghana suffered private investment slowdown because of the demand contraction associated with external adjustments. A number of monetary policies were introduced between the 1990s and 2000s. The Economic Emergency Act of 1987 was one of the policies that contributed to the sluggish growth in private investment during this period. Because of the huge competition that existed between public and private sectors for funding, some economic policies crowded out private investment in lieu of public sector borrowing.

CHAPTER 3

Gross Domestics Products and Government Expenditures

Private Investment and Gross Domestic Products

The information provided in this chapter represents the real GDP of Sierra Leone from 1980 to 2015 compared to the private investment for the same period. As discussed earlier, investment fluctuations can present major sources in national income stability, and vice versa. However, whether it is the acquirement of capital assets, growth in human capital, or the formation of new production ability, investment is a vehicle for economic growth, and economic growth also provides the same vehicle for the development of the private investment.

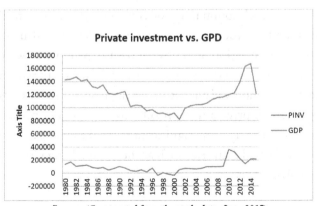

Source: (Constructed from the study data, June 2017)

The diagram shows a fall in the RGDP to private investment from 1981 to 1995. The ratio was at its lowest in 1997 and 2000. After the 2 per cent increase in the RGDP to private investment ratio in 1981, the contribution of private investment to the RGDP continued to fall until after 2009, when an 8 per cent increase in private investment contributed a total of 9 per cent to the RGDP, and in 2010, when there was a massive 254 per cent jump in private investment. The result of the boom in the mining sector contributed 30 per cent to the RGDP in the country. Even though the RGDP to private investment ratio fell from 17 per cent to 8 per cent in 2013, private investment contributed 13 per cent and 18 per cent to real gross domestic product in 2014 and 2015, respectively. The country's private investment began to pick up after the fall in the global iron ore price and the Ebola outbreak.

After the war in 2002, Sierra Leone made some efforts towards promoting private investment. The country was able to make some reforms in both the public and private sectors. A number of international and indigenous business erupted, including the telecommunication companies, the commercial banks, and microcredit institutions. Foreign investment, foreign aid, inflation, and government expenditures were the key drivers of economic growth. In Ghana, tax reform systems and improved budget management were used as tools to strengthen private investment. Contribution of private investment to GDP was significantly small as compared to other developed countries such as the United Kingdom and the United States.

Private Investment and Government Recurrent Expenditure

Recurrent expenditures include salaries made to public sector workers, utilities, and other consumables.

The government recurrent expenditure curve shows the spread between private investment and government recurrent expenditures from 1980 to 2015. Private investment increased sharply from 1980 to 1981. Government recurrent expenditure in Sierra Leone fell by 24 per cent in the same period but rose again in 1982 by 20 per cent. The steepest point in the 1980s was in 1987 and 1988, when recurrent expenditures fell by 23 per cent and 42 per cent, respectively.

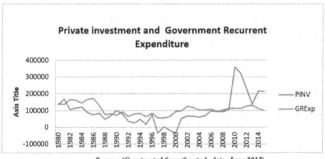

Source: (Constructed from the study data, June 2017)

Private investment fell by 45 per cent in 1988 after an initial rise by 14 per cent in the previous years. However, both the private investment and government recurrent expenditure curves show a decline from 1980 to the early 2000s, when both variables began rising, especially between 2000 and 2002. This was the period after the war, when Sierra Leone declared peace. Statistics suggest that investors and government responded to the end of the war by injecting money in the form of government utilities and salaries. Government recurrent expenditure increased because of some reforms in the public sector immediately after the war in 2010.

Over these years, the government made insignificant strides to reduce poverty by increasing income, offering better access to education, and attempting to improve health services across the country. These activities triggered government recurrent expenditures between 2003 and 2010. Available statistics from the Ministry of Finance suggest that the recurrent expenditure in Sierra Leone has always been higher than capital expenditure. Government expenditure was difficult to control especially after the war, when there was so much need for reconstruction, though most of the funding came from donor governments and institutions.

Private Investments and Government Development Expenditure

Government development expenditure could also attribute to the model based on economic theory. An increase in government development expenditure has the propensity of improving the existing infrastructure in the economy. Upgrading the existing infrastructure will stimulate private investment because businesses will have the opportunity to accumulate stock and form capital.

Changes in government expenditure portfolio affects private investment because public and private capital formation can have crown-in effects. A series of studies argued that decreases in public investment in the United States can explain the post-1970 productivity slowdown. In Sierra Leone's case, the nearby graph shows a very strong relationship between the movements in private investment and government investment curves. Both curves show slopes from 1980 to 1996 and from 1998 to 2000. The private investment and government expenditure curves were flat between 2005 and 2008, indicating a slowdown in government expenditure, which in an ordinary sense affected private investment. However, like other fiscal variables, the government increased development expenditure after 2010, and the intention was to stimulate growth.

The following table shows the private investment and government development expenditure curves from 1980 to 2015.

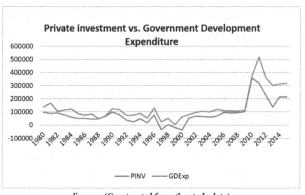

Source: (Constructed from the study data)

Even though the drop in private investment was deeper than the drop in government development expenditure after 1988, private investment jumped from a previous 46 per cent fall in 1987 to a 45 per cent rise in 1989, whereas government development expenditure jumped from 1 per cent to 52 per cent in the same period. In this same period, private expenditure as a percentage of government development expenditure fell slightly, from 101 per cent to 97 per cent. The similarity in behaviour of both curves is evidenced throughout the period. When government development expenditure rose sharply from 42 per cent fell in 1995 to a 151 per cent rise in 1996, private investment also jumped from a 61 per cent fall to a 311 per cent rise. The biggest rise in private investment was from 8 per cent in 2009 to 254 per cent in 2010, during the iron ore investment boom. This also triggered a sharp rise in government development expenditure from 5 per cent to 232 per cent in 2010 at a time when the elasticity of private investment was 96 per cent of government investment.

In the case of Ghana, Pickson (2016) pointed out that private sector investment slide during the 1980s, from 8.0 per cent in 1975 to 2.9 per cent in 1983 and from 4.4 per cent in 1984 to 2.5 per cent in 1992. Subsequently, investment in the private sector increased from 2.5 per cent in 1992 to 12.7 per cent in 2000 and from 16.7 per cent in 2001 to 17.0 per cent in 2005. This eventually declined to 6.0 per cent in 2013. This trend prompted several fiscal policy drives by the government of Ghana aiming at improving private sector investment.

The gloomy performance of private investment in Ghana was inconsistent with the growth of government investment as a percentage of GDP, which grew from 3.4 per cent in 1970 to

7.4 per cent in 1976 and afterwards fell to 0.9 per cent in 1983. After 1983, Ghana realized a steady growth in government investment. The country's development expenditure expanded from 2.5 per cent in 1984 to 10.3 per cent in 1992, and government expenditure increased at an average of 11 per cent between 1992 and 2004 and continued to improve to 24.5 per cent in 2012, before it finally fell to 16.7 per cent in 2013. Unlike Sierra Leone, where there are signs of a positive relationship between private investment and government development expenditure, the performance in Ghana has not shown a satisfactory response (Aduna and Akupalu 2014). Most of the accessible literature on the study of government investment in Ghana concentrated on economic growth and fiscal policy in general rather than paying attention to the specific issues, such as the existing relationship between government investment expenditure and private investment.

The problem in Ghana and especially in Sierra Leone is the lack of sufficient empirical evidence to explain the reasons for the changes in government development expenditure other than simple budgetary reasons.

Private Investment and Total Government Spending

The result shows that government spending has influenced private investment in the economy of Sierra Leone, both domestic and foreign direct investment. In the long run, the balance between private investment and public spending is one very important fiscal debate. Critics of the Keynesian school oppose any form of government intervention, in the form of spending to enhance growth in the economy and stimulating private sector growth, because they believe that increased government spending will increase the size of the public sector, making it more complex. Proponents of the Keynesian school hold on to the opinion that government spending will enhance private sector growth and push the economy towards full employment.

In Sierra Leone, the toll on the financial system, productive ability, and infrastructure set the pace for huge government spending, especially after the civil conflict. Before the conflict in the 1980s and early 1990s, economic yields were an annual average of 1.8 per cent. According to the World Bank (2007a), the country's official economy fell by almost 40 per cent between 1990 and 1999. The nearby figure shows the private investment and total government curves from 1980 to 2015.

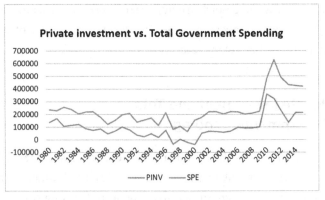

Source: (Constructed from the study data)

After the civil war, the government of Sierra Leone committed to a recovery programme to enable economic and social development of the countryside. The introduction of the PRSP outlined various challenges within the private and the public sectors and suggested various strategies to address them. Nevertheless, the rate of unskilled labour, the size of the country's domestic market, challenging infrastructure, and undiversified economic composition continue to delay progress in economic and social reforms. During this period, the government invested a lot in recovery programmes and rebuilding the infrastructure through the Social Action for Poverty Alleviation (SAPA), which later changed to National Commission for Social Action (NaCSA).

The curve shows the relationship between private investment and government spending in Sierra Leone form 1980 to 2015. Government spending was larger than private investment in all years under the study. More important, the figure shows a strong relationship between government spending and private investment given to the literature of the Keynesian school. Apart from the negative relationship from 1980 to 1984, when private investment rose by 24 per cent and government spending fell by 4 per cent in 1981, government expenditure picked up again by 12 per cent in 1982 while private investment fall in the same period by 37 per cent. The increase in government expenditure in 1980 was a result of the hosting of the Organisation of African Unity (OAU), under the presidency of Dr Siaka P. Stevens. Sierra Leone invested in infrastructures, including roads and airport. Government spending fall sharply after the OAU, giving a sudden fall in private investment, which had begun to pick up during the OAU. Sierra Leone faced a very turbulent economic situation thereafter. Both private investment and government expenditure continued to fall until 1996, when government expenditure and private investment increased by 86 per cent and 311 per cent, respectively, at a time when private investment was 35 per cent of government spending. The same trend repeated during the years but was also very conspicuous in 2010, when government spending increased by 118 per cent and private investment increased by 224 per cent, resulting in a 96 per cent relationship between private investment and government spending. Economic experts argue that there has been a big shift in the opportunity cost of investing in developing countries such as Sierra Leone due to the huge fiscal challenges, especially the public budget constraints in improving government spending, especially when global commodity prices such as iron ore, oil, and gold are falling (Clilihber 1990). During the early 1980s and 1990s, growing corruption, especially in the diamond business, seriously damaged the institutionalization of the economy. This caused institutions and businesses to collapse, and the sluggish trends of private investment and government spending in the economy triggered the civil war in 2002.

Sierra Leone became politically stable and reestablished political order after the September 2007 elections, where the presidential candidate of the political opposition, Alhaji Dr Ahmed Tejan Kabba, peacefully took over the government. This political change was important, especially for foreign direct investment and confidence in the future of Sierra Leone economic change. The new government continued to trigger development but paid more attention to education, employment, transformation infrastructure and institutions, poverty reduction, and improving the administrative competence of government policies sectors. During this process, government spending increased, and foreign direct investment were also attracted, especially in the financial services and mining sectors. During the last quarter of the study, government expenditure and private investment increased because of the political and economic stability in Sierra Leone. The country also witnessed the implementation of two other policy reform documents, the Agenda for Change (PRSP II) and the Amender for Prosperity. The focus of these documents is to reduce poverty and stimulate economic growth. The latter part of the study stated that especially after 2010, the country's concentration in mining sector drove economic growth until 2014, when the price of iron ore fell by almost 80 per cent. There is currently huge interest in agriculture, where government has dedicated lots of resources.

The size of government can also be determined by the country's total government spending. Results from a study by Adu et al. (2014) reveal that long-run analysis on fiscal variables and government expenditure show it takes much longer for government expenditure to transform into positive benefits for the Ghanaian economy. This means that the government can decide to increase government spending to promote private investment, and hence economic growth. The results might take much longer than expected depending on other economic, social, and political characteristics in the economy. "Because government expenditure has a direct positive relationship with real GDP growth, it utilization to trigger economic growth and improves investment in the private sector" (Adu et al. 2014). Studies have suggested that the government can take other fiscal policy measures other than increasing government expenditure if it wishes to trigger economic growth and boost private investment in the short term. Fiscal policy literature supports the fact that policymakers can seek to prevent the crowding-out effect by taking into consideration the interests of the private sector when scheming for the expenditure section that competes with the private sector.

After the early 1990s, the country's policy sector carefully considered promoting sectors such as agriculture and financial services to trigger high productivity in the private sector. However, corruption in Sierra Leone has an effect on the optimal outcome of public sector management, which in turn cascades to private sector development. There is a need to ensure that monies provided through government expenditure mechanisms for productive activities are used for those activities in order to produce growth in the local private sector. There have been calls for the government to make sure that government expenditure meant to boost private investments is provided directly to private sector institutions through subsidies or other forms of direct investment. "This could be achieved by enforcing the local content law on all contract awarded to foreign firms and also through private public partnerships" (Adu et al. 2014).

CHAPTER 4

Private Consumption

Private Investment and Private Consumption

Private consumption measures the volume of household expenditure in the economy. Like firms and the government, individual households constitute an integral part of the country's economic development. Proponents of fiscal policy believe that the level of private investment in the economy can be interpreted to an extent regarding the level of private consumption in the economy. Government spending need not to be seen only as focusing on infrastructural development and meeting government recurrent budget demands, but also as a measure to stimulate growth by encouraging direct household spending.

Economists and financial experts believe that an increase in private consumption will boost private investment in the long run if investors take advantage of the boost and the policy environment is responding to the need. However, both empirical and theological literature have questioned the assumption that short-term fiscal multipliers are always positive in the short or long run. From a theoretical perspective, it has also been suggested that the risk impact and weak market hypothesis might have a negative private investment impact in the short term even when private consumption is growing.

The curve shows the relationship private investment and private consumption form 1980 to 2015.

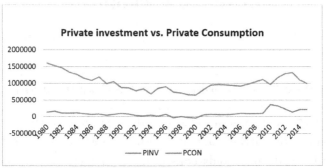

Source: (Constructed from the study data)

According to statistics, private consumption observed a deep fall from 1980 to 1996 by an average of 7 per cent and then a 17 per cent fall from 1987 to 1988, even after a 9 per cent growth in the previous years. This shows that private consumption is an important variable for private investment. It has been suggested that unstable private consumption is not a good signal for fiscal balance in the economy.

In Sierra Leone, the biggest growth of 24 per cent in the private consumption variable occurred in 1995 and 2001, at a time when private investment fell by 61 per cent and 242 per cent, respectively. This does not show a good relationship between the two variables, even though these were not the years with the largest private consumption portfolios. Total private consumption has been greater than private investment in the economy, which is normal for economic theory, but the spread has not been appreciable. The research reveals instances where private investment was as little as 2 per cent, and private consumption was 0 per cent. The two curves more or less responded similarly in different fiscal periods except from 2012 to 2015, when there was a greater spread in the curves.

The number of empirical literature addressing the long-term and short-term effects of fiscal policy, especially in developing countries, is increasing. Some Keynesian economists believe that public expenditure has little effect on private consumption. They believe that private wealth net of government debt has a big influence on private consumption in an economy. Keynesian researchers also outline several fiscal variables that can positively influence private consumptions; some of these include government transfers to household net of interest payments and government expenditure for the payment of interest on public debt and total income. These variables, in turn, have a negative effect on taxes and retained earnings.

The literature has been able to associate fiscal variables to private investments and consumption. Private consumption can trigger a sharp turn in private investment in the economy, but if other fiscal variables are left unchecked, it will further trigger widespread effects on inflation, real interest rates, and even government spending in the economy.

Like the Keynesians, Ricardian economists believes that government expenditure for interest payments on domestic and external debt has very little effect on private consumption in the economy, whereas government transfers to households do influence private consumptions.

In the case of Ghana, empirical models have suggested that government expenditure has no impact on private consumption, but private consumption influences private investment. According to Pickson (2016), the hypothesis of the relationship between private investment and private consumption was accepted, and actual trade taxes did not have an impact on actual private consumption in Ghana between 1970 and 2004. However, studies have shown that actual direct taxes had a negative impact on real private consumption in the same period.

CHAPTER 5

Domestic Revenue Mobilization

Instruments of Revenue Mobilization

The fiscal discipline of a government is often reflected in its national budgets. Although a budget deficit in a particular year may not accurately construe how government performs in that year, generally, consistent surpluses and deficits tend to show disciplined fiscal policy (or lack thereof). In Sierra Leone, like most African countries, budget deficits have made their mark for most of the 1980s and 1990s, and even in recent years. With the budget showing red ink most of these years, it would be difficult to make the economic improvements that are needed to attract and stimulate the demand of foreign investors. For example, budget deficits expressed as a percentage of GDP have remained high since the first half of the 1990s in countries such as Kenya and Zimbabwe (Pigato 2001).

Taxes have been fundamental to government revenue mobilization, and although governments are keen to diversify their economics, it is clear that the situation will maintain the status quo for a long time.

Private Investment and Total Tax Revenue

Total government taxes includes, but are not limited to, the following: corporate income tax on the net incomes of corporate entities in Sierra Leone, charged at a rate of 30 per cent on the net profit on minimum chargeable income basis; GST, an indirect tax charged on the domestic consumption of goods and services, levied at each stage in the chain of manufactured, and distributed from the state of raw materials to the final sale, based on the value added at each stage; excise duty, a domestic tax on the production and sale of a commodity locally; and import duty, levied on the custom insurance and freight (CIF) value of imports by the fiscal authorities of a country to raise state revenue or to protect domestic industries from efficient or predatory foreign competitors. The curve shows the total tax revenue, indirect taxes, and personal income tax and corporation tax curves from 1980 to 2015.

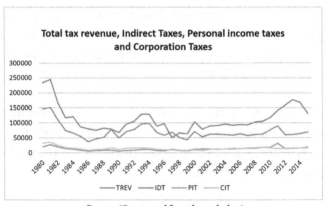

Source: (Constructed from the study data)

The tax rates in Sierra Leone have been changing to enhance fiscal balance and meet regional economic integration. Foreign and domestic companies are subjected to 30 per cent corporation tax rate, except for mining companies, which pay 35 per cent of their profit chargeable to corporation tax. Personal income tax ranged from 20 per cent to 30 per cent before January 2016. The current maximum personal income tax threshold was adjusted to 35 per cent after January 2016. Sierra Leone adopted the common external tariff, which set four tariff bands at 0 per cent, 5 per cent, 10 per cent, and 20 per cent. Other taxes include the diamond tax at 5 per cent, and this also applied to royalties for artisanal licenses of holders of precious stones. Precious metals are taxed at 3 per cent of their value, as are other minerals. The following figure shows the private investment and total tax revenue curves from 1980 to 2015.

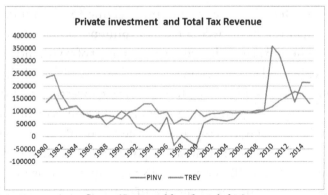

Source: (Constructed from the study data)

Unlike most of the other variables in this book, data for total tax revenue and private investment from 1980 to 2015 have not shown an impressive result. Private investment was

146 per cent of total tax revenue. The graph shows that the TTR and PI curves are closer compared to other variables in the study, even though there is a period with a large spread between 1990 and 1997. The spread shows that tax collected exceeded private investment in the economy, and this trend continued until 2002. Private investment showed negative results during these periods, and the biggest spread was between 2009 and 2012, during the iron ore boom. The economic assumption suggested that total tax revenue should increase as private investment increases, if there is a robust tax collection system in the economy and if there are little or no tax breaks in the economy. During the investment boom between 2009 and 2014, most of the mining companies enjoyed tax exemptions.

In Sierra Leone, there is a growing debate over the significance of tax incentives to boost private investment especially when the tax incentive giving to the mining companies have accounted for billions of leones of uncollected taxes. The economic argument of tax incentives goes beyond just protecting infant industries, but also helps governments to attract foreign direct investment. Tax incentives are provided to encourage foreign investment in the economy, this is granted at the rate of 40 per cent for the first year on all plants and equipments, other items are depreciated at 10 per cent to 15 per cent rate depending on the item and its economic life. A loss carry forward provision of 50 per cent of the previous year's taxable income is also provided to strengthen private investment in Sierra Leone. Another reason why government often gives tax incentives is to encourage companies to invest in economically dejected part of a country. This is not likely the case for Sierra Leone.

In Sierra Leone, like most sub-Saharan African countries, tax policies have been used as a tool to promote investment in some sectors. However, results have not proven any strong relationship between tax incentives and private investments growth. Because dependence on tax policies to influence investment spending did not feature prominently, Sierra Leone has also been using the scheme to increase export earnings. The country has introduced some of the biggest tax breaks in the subregion and has been criticized for not playing a rational revenue mobilization game.

Private Investment and Indirect Taxes

Economists have suggested that the total of all taxes on domestic goods has a negative relationship to private investment. This is because a significant amount of the capital will be used to pay taxes and hence crowd out private investment. Unlike excise duties, import duties are levied on the value of imports into a country. They are collected by the customs department at the port of entry. Other than to raise revenue, import duties can also be used as a tool to protect domestic produced goods against international competition. The relationship between import duty and private investment can either be positive or negative because these taxes increase prices and hence reduce demand and private investment in the long term. The GST, similarly known as value added taxes in some countries, is levied as a percentage of goods and services that fall under the category.

Unlike other taxes, GST has a strong relationship with inflation because increased taxes tend to increase prices, and hence inflation. The curve in the following figure shows the private investment and total tax revenue curves of Sierra Leone from 1980 to 2015.

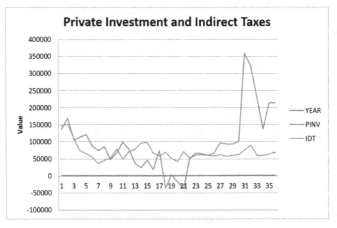

Source: (Constructed from the study data)

The total portfolio on private investment and total indirect taxes shows similar results with the total tax revenue spread. This is because indirect taxes contributed more to the total tax revenue than another form of taxes. The average proportion of indirect taxes to total tax revenue from 1980 to 2015 was approximately 68 per cent, given the fact that the government can strengthen tax generation by designing and enforcing robust measures to collect all taxes within the indirect tax bracket. The indirect tax curve is flatter than the total tax curve, with more narrow spreads along the private investment curve, compared to the spread between total tax revenue and private investment. After the 16 per cent growth in 2002, indirect tax collection showed a sluggish response until after 2009, when private investment had a big boost from the mining sector, and then indirect taxes rose from 2 per cent in 2009 to 24 per cent in 2010. In some periods, total indirect tax portfolios were greater than the total portfolio of private investment in the economy, especially between 1992 and 2000, when private investment showed negative growth.

Private Investment and Personal Income Taxes

This is a compulsory tax imposed on income of individuals and companies. It was calculated by adding all the taxes that fall under this category. The curve below shows the private investment and personal income tax curves of Sierra Leone from 1980 to 2015.

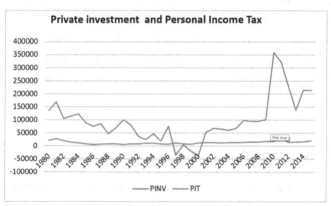

Source: (Constructed from the study data)

Personal income tax (PIT) contributed very little to total tax revenue as compared to other forms of taxes. Personal income taxes did not change much between 1984 and 1999, and that is why the PIT curve has been very flat. The spread with the PINV curve is also more than the total tax revenue and the indirect tax curves. Personal income tax picked up in 2000 after the war at 24 per cent, and the highest was 76 per cent in 2011, when the iron ore boom promoted employment in the economy. Economic theory suggested that the slope of the income tax curve is highly proportional to the employment curve, meaning personal income tax will increase as employment in the economy increases, provided that employers are making the correct pay as you earn (PAYE) for their employees.

In Ghana, results have shown that personal income tax increases with private investment. Results from the study of Kapur et al. (1991) suggested that economic decline from 1970 to 1982 crippled private sector growth, which in turn had a negative effect on employment, so personal taxes shrunk conspicuously. However, Ghana was able to introduce strong policy measures in the late 1990s, which enhanced some of the challenges in private investment growth and in turn improved employment and personal taxes.

Private Investment and Corporation Tax

Corporate income tax, on the net incomes of corporate entities in Sierra Leone, was charged at a rate of 30 per cent on the net profit on minimum chargeable income basis. The curve in the following figure shows the private investment and corporation tax curves of Sierra Leone from 1980 to 2015.

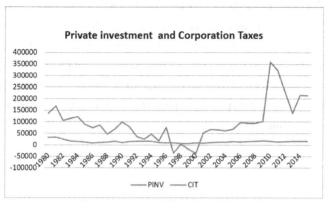

Source:·(Constructed·from·the·study·data)

As previously stated, theoretically, the relationship between corporate income tax and private investment is expected to be negative. This is as a result of the fact that a high corporate income tax rate will serve as a disincentive to private investment because the lion's share of the net profit that could have been ploughed back into the business will now be used to pay the high corporate tax.

The corporation tax curve is as flat as the personal income tax curve with similar spreads. Total corporation tax in the economy was far below the private investment curve except from 1997 to 2000, when the private investment portfolio was negative. The changes in corporation tax rate greatly influenced the amount of tax collected from corporate institutions. Meanwhile, research has also proven that a broader tax base can help increase tax collection even when tax rates are lower. The result presented in the graph is similar with all the other fiscal variables when the spread between private investment and corporation tax curves from 2009 to 2014 is considered. Private investment grew at an average of 56 per cent, whereas corporation tax fell from 7 per cent in 2013 to 1 per cent in 2014, even when private investment was at its highest. This is the same period when prefinancing the mining sector through external debt was very difficult to obtain because mining companies were the major taxpayers in the economy.

PART 2

Discussion and Descriptive Statistical Analysis of Financial Sector Development in Sierra Leone

CHAPTER 6

Introduction of Financial Sector Development in Sierra Leone

Brief Overview

The ratio of financial asset to GDP has been widely used to define financial asset in an economy. Theoretical economic and financial literatures have argued that resources would be efficiently allocated when the financial sector is effective. This in turn would ignite other variables (such as interest rate reduction) that would promote economic growth. Meanwhile, there has been mixed opinion as to the extent to which the financial sector promotes economic growth.

The financial sector of any economy is the composition of both the money and capital market—that is, the total number of institutions, markets, and other monetary securities (instruments) that are present in a particular country. Added to this is the legal and regulatory framework that allows the establishment of contracts and the execution of transactions through the multiplication of credits to ensure a prudent, safe, and sound financial system. In context, the entity concept is applied as wealth control, and ownership is driven by the financial system. Economic growth, strength, and size are dependent on the financial sector of the economy as a whole (Al-Yousif 2002). The financial sector includes businesses that offer multiple services, such as insurance, banking, brokerage, accountancy, and other government-sponsored activities. Other financial sector activities consist of hedge fund, venture capitalist, and conglomerate activities. On the other hand, the financial sector development is the aggregate number of financial securities (instruments) and institutions, as well as the sophistication, interrelationship, establishment, and growth of such institutions. It includes all the financial services providers within an economy.

Financial sector institutions are expected to perform best at times when interest rates are set low. The biggest revenue source of the financial sector in Sierra Leone comes from interest received from loans, insurance premiums, and other major investments in the financial system. In Sierra Leone, it has been observed that the more public projects are undertaken, the more loan creation is made by financial organizations.

The role of the financial sector in any economy is important to the financial and economic development of that particular country. For instance, commercial banks serve as intermediaries in the money market. Acting between those with excess cash and those in deficit occurs as people deposit savings to the bank, and banks in turn give it as loans to other interested parties (credit) for a fixed period of time with interest.

Some of the functions of financial systems are facilitation of trade diversification, monitoring of investments, mobilization and pooling of savings, investment and allocation of capital, corporate governance and regulation of the financial market, promotion of exchanges of goods and services, and risk management.

In order for financial sector development to occur, financial markets (money and capital) and instruments (shares, bonds, and derivatives) must collectively work to reduce enforcement, information generation, and transaction cost. It is the most important economic development tool that drives job creation and wealth.

Financial sector development programmes are undertaken by the government to ensure that enough savings, inflow of foreign direct investment, job creation, and business expansion is achieved and that poverty is reduce.

The importance of financial sectors, particularly in solving transaction cost and information asymmetry, cannot be overemphasized. Financial sectors play a vital role in the mobilization of savings; facilitating trade, diversification, and pooling of risks; monitoring firms and exerting corporate governance; and facilitating exchange. The finance-growth nexus has attracted series of research over the years, with most authors highlighting the accumulation of physical and human capital and the total factor productivity growth as the major channels through which financial development affects overall economic growth (Levine 1997). This chapter is motivated by the basis that despite all the empirical works, this topic remains highly contested.

The components of the financial system in Sierra Leone and in most emerging market economies are made up of discount houses, insurance companies, and the commercial banking institutions, and even of nonformal financial institutions such as microcredit. However, the Sierra Leone financial system is, to a very large extent, underdeveloped due to the adoption of financially repressive policies, political corruption and poor macroeconomic management, and bank malfeasance, giving rise to insolvency, low savings rates, and insufficient resource allocation.

Financial Sector Development

In this book, public sector ratio is otherwise used as a measure for financial sector development. It is the most comprehensive indicator of the activities of the deposit money banks, and it is calculated as the amount of domestic credit allocated to the private sector by the commercial banking sector divided by real GDP. Private sector ratio also indicates the extent to which the banking sector finances the economy and more specifically the extent to which commercial banks finance private investment and private sector development. According to the World Bank, domestic credit provided to the private sector includes financial resources which establish a claim for repayment, such as loans, purchases of nonequity securities, trade credits, and other amounts receivables. These domestic credits exclude credits extended to government and public enterprises (Beck and Levine 2004). The following figure shows the private sector credit ratio curve of Sierra Leone from 1980 to 2015.

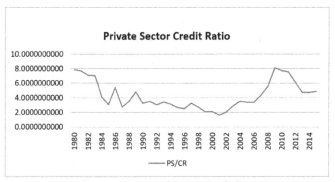

Source:·(Constructed·from·the·study·data)

The ratio of private sector credit increases by an average of 2 per cent from 1980 to 2015. The results from the diagram shows the biggest increase of 75 per cent in 1986 and the largest slide of 49 per cent in 1987. The volume of credit given by the commercial banks was encouraging between 2007 and 2009, but it fell sharply afterwards and picked up slightly in 2015. Banks' credit to the private sector is an important indicator of financial sector development and therefore shows the strength of the financial system. Arguably, the more deposits the banks receives, the better it is in a position to provide private sector credit and promote domestic investment. The following curve shows the private sector credit ratio in Ghana from 1980 to 2014.

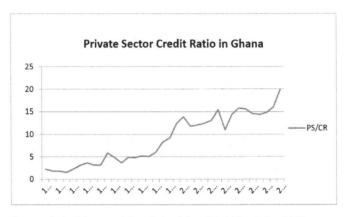

Source (derived from statistics obtained from World Bank data 2017)

The diagram represents the credit to private sector as a percentage of GDP in Ghana from 1960 to 2014. In 2014, Ghana gives the highest credit to the private sector, 20 per cent expressed in GDP, whereas the lowest (1.5 per cent) was realized in 1983. Monitoring of debtors, information, and management of credit risks were three important tools identified as responsible for the 2014 credit penetration (Ahiawodzi 2013). When credit risk is properly managed, the default risk of banks will be low, and banks will generally benefit from lower NPL, which is a very strong indicator for financial sector development in an economy.

The case of Ghana is an example to guide credits in the financial sector for the promotion of private investment.

CHAPTER 7

Private Sector Credit, Real Interest Rate, Money Supply, and Inflation

Change in Private Sector Credit versus Change in Real Interest Rates

The decline in the demand for credit will consequently limit the size of the financial sector by reducing the flow of credit to the private sector. The reverse is the case when real interest rates are low. The curve in the following figure shows the private sector credit ratio and real interest rates curves of Sierra Leone from 1980 to 2015.

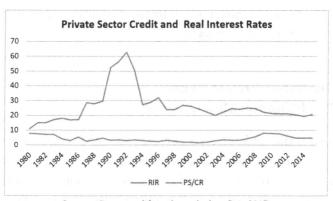

Source: (Constructed from the study data, June 2017)

The curve shows a relatively negative relationship between real interest rates and the private sector credit ratio. The biggest change in the real exchange rate of 77 per cent in 1990 was at a time when private sector credit decreased by 33 per cent, whereas the biggest increase in private sector credit of 45 per cent in 2009 was at a time when real interest rate fell by 10 per cent.

Even though the result does not show smooth percentage changes during the period, private sector credit is almost always increasing when the real interest rate is falling, except in 2015, when Sierra Leone was just recovering from the Ebola crisis.

In his study, Ahiawodzi (2013) examines interest rate liberalization in Ghana from 1970 to 2013 and suggests that commercial banks still rationalize credit even when interest rates are liberalized. This is because credit in the financial sector is affected not only by interest rates but also by adverse selection and moral hazard.

Change in Private Sector Credit versus Money Supply

This is the entire stock of currency and other liquid assets in a country's economy as of a particular time. The supply of money takes account of cash, coins, and balances held in savings and current accounts. Money supply data is collected, recorded, and published periodically, typically by the Central Bank. The theoretical relationship between money supply and financial sector development is such that growth in money has a tendency of fuelling inflation, which consequently reduces the value of money and discourages savings and financial intermediation. The resulting decline in aggregate savings will limit the ability of commercial banks in extending credit to the public, which consequently inhibits financial sector development. The curve in the following figure shows the private sector credit ratio and the money supply curves of Sierra Leone from 1980 to 2015.

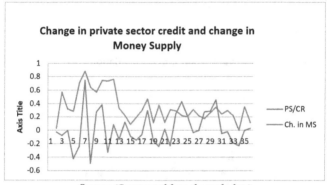

Source: (Constructed from the study data)

The changes in money supply for the period exceed the amount given to the private sector as credit by commercial banks, with the exception of 2002 and from 2010 to 2015. The biggest increase in money supply was in 1991, when money supply increased by 76 per cent in the private sector and credit increased by 38 per cent in the same period. The spread between money supply and private sector credit was wider in the first half of the period, and the later period shows some significant changes. This suggests that during the first half of the elasticity between the change in money supply and private sector, credit was elastic.

Research has suggested that implemented financial policy failed in Sierra Leone in the 1980s and 1990s, enhanced resources for economic growth, and also left a thin financial system with little room for growth.

Private Sector Credit and Inflation

The following figure shows the private sector credit ratio and inflation curves for Sierra Leone from 1980 to 2015.

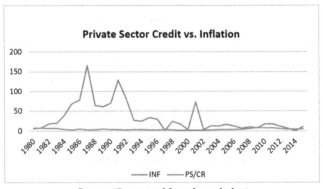

Source:·(Constructed·from·the·study·data)

The change in inflation was far more proportional than the change in private sector credit. This makes the change in the private sector credit curve flat, even though the change in the inflation curve has also been relatively flat, except in 1998, 2001, and 2015, when there was an exponential change in inflation percentage, as compared to the 16 per cent fall in 1998, the 23 per cent fall in 2001, and the 3 per cent fall in private sector credit for the same period. The behaviour of the curve supported the empirical argument, which suggested that increased inflation would urge the government to reduce the amount of money in circulation by urging banks to reduce the amount of credit given to the private sector. Not much attention has been paid to fiscal policy on financial development. The role of government debt in developing financial sectors in Sierra Leone shows that inflation and financial repression are detrimental to financial sector development and growth. The country therefore needs to advocate for policy measures that can control inflation in the economy in general. This will reduce interest rates and hence increase the credit given to the private sector by banks.

REFERENCES

Ackah, I. and Adu, F. (2015). *Government Expenditure and Economic Growth Dynamics in Ghana*. Research Gate Page. http://www.researchgate.net/publication/27033848.

Adam, C. 1998. *Macroeconomic Management: New Methods and Policy Issues, Time Series Econometrics for Developing Countries*. New York: Oxford University Press.

Adugna, H. 2013. "Determinants of Private Investment in Ethiopia". *Journal of Economics and Sustainable Development*, 4/20, 186–194.

Afonso, A., Ebert, W., Schuknecht, L., and Thone, M. 2005. "Quality of Public Finances and Growth". Working Paper Series No. 438, European Central Bank.

African Economic Outlook. 2009. *Country Notes Vol. 1 and 2 OECD 2009*. OECD Publishing.

African Economic Outlook. 2017. *African Microeconomics Prospects*. http://www.africaneconomicoutlook.org/en/outlook/africa-s-macoreconomic-prospect.

Ahuja, H. L. 2007. *Macro Economics Theory and Policy: Advance Analysis*. New Delhi: S. Chand.

Akpalu, W. 2002. "Modelling Private Investment in Ghana: An Empirical Time Series Econometrics Investigation (1970–1994)". *The Ogua Journal of Social Sciences*, 4.

Alesina, A., Ardagna S., and Perotti, R. 2002. "Fiscal Policy, Profits, and Investment". *American Economic Review,* 92/3, 571–89.

Alie, J. A. D. 2010. *History of Sierra Leone,* revised edition. http://www.amazon.com/A-New-History-Sierra-Leone/dp/0333519841.

Al-Yousif, K. 2002. "Financial Development and Economic Growth: Another Look at the Evidence from Developing Countries". *Review of Financial Economic,* 11/2, 131–50.

Andrianova, S., and Demetriades, P. 2008. "Sources and Effectiveness of Financial Development: What We Know and What We Need to Know". In B. Guha-Khasnobis and G. Mavrotas (eds.), *Financial Development, Institutions, Growth and Poverty Reduction,* UNU-WIDER Studies in Development Economics and Policy.

Anthony K., Ahiawodzi1, A. K., Gyimah, F., and Sackey. 2013. *Determinants of Credit Rationing to the Private Sector in Ghana.* Institute of Professional Studies, Accra, Ghana. Catholic University College of Ghana, Fiapre, Ghana.

Arrow, K. 1968. "Optimal Capital Policy with Irreversible Investment". In John Hicks and J. Wolfe (eds.), *Value, Capital, and Growth Essays,* University of Edinburg.

Aryeetey et al. 2000. "Operationalising Pro-Poor Growth". Working Paper, a joint initiative of AFD, BMZ (GTZ, KfW Development Bank), DFID, and the World Bank.

Asante, Y. 2000. "Determinants of Private Investment Behaviour in Ghana". African Economic Research Consortium Research Paper No. 100, Nairobi: AERC, Mlambo and Oshikay.

Aschauer, D. A. 1985. "Fiscal Policy and Aggregate Demand". *American Economics Review*, 75/1, 117–27.

Aschauer, D. A. 1989. "Does Public Capital Crowd-out Private Capital?" *Journal of Monetary Economics*, 24/2, 171–88.

Assibey, E. O., Bokpin, G. A., and Twerefou, D. K. 2012. "Microenterprise Financing Preference: Testing POH within the Context of Ghana's Rural Financial Market". *Journal of Economic Studies*, 39/1, 84–105.

Atesoglu, H. S., and Emerson, J. 2008. "Fiscal Policy, Profit and Investment: Some Additional Evidence". *Applied Economics Letters. Autoregressive Models.* New York: Oxford University Press.

Bank of Ghana. 2013. "Central Bank Bulletin". IDPS Department Bank of Ghana.

Bank of Sierra Leone. 2008. Bulletin.

Bawumia, M., and Danso, T. O. 2008. "Ghana's Reforms Transforms Its Financial Sector". *African Financial Reforms.*

Becker, E., and Stevenson, R. W. 2005. "Fiscal Policy Theory". *New York Times* (10 June).

Becker, G. 1962. "Investment in Human Capital: A Theoretical Approach". *Journal of Political Economy*, 70, 9–14.

Bende-Nabende, A. 2002. "Foreign Direct Investment Determinants in Sub-Sahara Africa: A Co-integration Analysis". The Business School, University of Birmingham.

Berg, A., Funke, N., and Hajdenberg A. 2009. "Fiscal Policy in Sub-Saharan African in Response to the Impact of the Global Crisis". IMF Staff Position Note, 14 May.

Better Investment. 2007. http://stage.betterinvesting.org/Public/default.

Bhatia, H. L. 1998. *Public Finance,* ninth edition. New Delhi: Vikas Publishing House.

Blair, Tony. 2006. "The United Kingdom Budget Debate". United Kingdom Parliamentary Debate Papers, May 2006.

Blejer, M. S., and Khan, M. S. 1984. "Government Policy and Private Investment in Developing Countries". *IMF Staff Papers,* 31/2, 379–403.

Bouakez, H., and Rebei, N. 2007. "Why Does Private Consumption Risk After a Government Spending Shock?" *Canadian Journal of Economics,* 40/3, 954–79.

Bradford, D., Jordan, Thomas, W., and Miller, J. 2009. *Fundamentals of Investment Valuation and Management,* fifth edition. Macmillan Press.

Buiter, W. H. 2001. "Note on Code for Fiscal Stability". *Oxford Economic Paper,* 53/1, 1–19.

Business Dictionary. 2013. http: businessdisctionary.com/ definition/expansionary-moneytary-policy.html.

Business Dictionary. 2014. www.businessdisctionary.com/ definition/expansionary-moneytary-policy.html.

Chhibber, A., and Dailami, M. 1990. "Fiscal Policy and Private Investment in Developing Countries, Recent Evidence on Key Selected Issues". WPS 559, Policy, Research and External Affairs, Development Economics Office of the Vice President, World Bank, December 1990.

Clilihber, A. 1990. "Fiscal Policy and Private Investment in Turkey". PPR Working Paper Series 120, World Bank.

Creswell, J. W. 2014. "A Conscience Introduction to Mixed Methods Research". Unpublished manuscript.

Crotty, J. R. 1990. *Owner-Manager Conflict and Financial Theories of Investment Instability: A Critical Assessment of Keynes.* Amherst, MA: Department of Economics, University of Massachusetts.

Crotty, J. R. 1993. *Rethinking Marxian Investment Theory: Keynes-Minsky Instability.* Amherst: MA: Department of Economics, University of Massachusetts, Amherst, Massachusetts. Third Revision: June 1992.

Davidson et al. 1978. "Econometric Modelling of the Aggregate Time-Series Relationship between Consumers' Expenditure and Income in the United Kingdom".

Dawson et al. 2006. "Reconsidering Qualitative and Qualitative Research Approaches: A Cognitive Development Perspective". *New Idea in Psychology*, 24, 229–39.

Dawson, G. 2002. "The Cost of Reducing Inflation". In H. Vane and B. Snowman (eds.), *An Encyclopedia of Microeconomics*, Aldershot: Edwaed Elgar.

Dawson, G., and Browne, V. 2006. *Macroeconomics and Economics Policy: Economic and Economic Change.* Open University Course DD202 team, 293.

Djankov, S., Ganser, T., and Ramalho, R. 2009. "The Effect of Corporate Taxes on Investment and Entrepreneurship". http://dx.doi.org/10.1257/mac.2.3.31.

Dunnings, J. H. 2001. "Paradigm of International Production: Past, Present and Future". *International Journal of Economics and Business.*

Economic Mecometer. http://mecometer.com/whats/sierra-leone/gdp-growth-rate.

Enders, W. 2004. *Applied Econometrics Time Series,* second edition. New York: John Wiley and Sons.

Engle, R. F., and Granger, C. W. J. 1987. "Co-integration and Error Correction". McMillan.

European Commission. 1990. "One Market One Money". *European Economy*. 44.

Evans, P., and Karras, G. 1994. "Are Government Activities Productive? Evidence from a Panel of US States". *Review of Economics and Statistics*, 76/1, 1–11.

Fazzari, S. M., and Cynamon, B. Z. 2008. "Household Debt in the Consumer Age: Source of Growth—Risk of Collapse". *Capitalist and Society*, 3/2.

Fontana, G. 2006. *Aggregate Demand Economic and Economic Change*. Open University Course DD202 team, 348.

Furceri, D., and Sousa, R. M. 2011. "The Impact of Government Spending on the Private Sector: Crowding-out versus Crowding-in Effect". *KYLKOS International Review for Social Sciences*.

Ghana National Revenue Authority. 2013. News Bulletin.

Ghana Statistics Services. 2013. *Ghana Macro Economic Policies 2013*.

Giavazzi, F., et al. 2000. "Saving Behaviour and the Effectiveness of Fiscal Policy". OECD Economic Outlook No. 76.

Giavazzi, F., Tullio, J., and Marco, P. 2000. "Searching for Non-linear Effects of Fiscal Policy: Evidence from Industrial and Developing Countries". *European Economic Review*, 44/7, 1259–89.

Gillis, M., Perkins, D. W., Roemer, M., and Sodgrass, D. R. 1987. *Economics of Development,* second edition. Norton.

Granger, C. W. J. 1987. "Cointegration and Error Correction: Representation, Estimation and Testing". *Econometrical,* 55, 251–276.

Hartman, David G. 1984. "Tax Policy and Foreign Direct Investment in the United States". *National Tax Journal,* 37/4, 475–88.

Hatz-Eakin, D. 1988. "Private Output, Government Capital and the Infrastructure 'Crisis'". Columbia University Discussion Paper No. 394, May 1988.

Hjelm, G. "2002. Effects of Fiscal Contractions: The Importance of Preceding Exchange Rate Movements". *The Scandinavian Journal of Economics,* 104/4, 423–41.

Hotz-Eakin. 1994. "A Smooth Ride". *The Economist* (18 March). http://www.google.com.sl/url?sa=t&rct=j&q=&esrc=s&source=web&cd=1&ved=0ahUKEwiq2KO5uJjVAhWLExoKHRfrD5kQFgggMAA&url=http%3A%2F%2Fwww.mbie.govt.nz%2Fpublications-research%2Fpublications%2Fecono mic-development%2F2006-occasional.

Hultan, C. R., and Schwab, R. M. 1991. "Public Capital Formation and Growth of Regional manufacturing Industries". *National Tax Journal,* 44/4, 121–34.

International Monetary Fund. 2014. *Annual Reports on Exchange Arrangements and Exchange Restrictions.*

https://www.google.com.sl/#q=International+Monetary+
Fund.+(2009);+Flexible+Exchange+Rates&spf=
1500628026387.

Jeff, D. O. 2007. *The Wall Street Journal: Complete Personal Finance Guidebook.*

Johansen, S. 1995. *Likelihood-Based Inference in Cointegrated Vector.* http://research-methodologydt.joansen/co-interationtech.

Johnson, E. G. 2011. "Financial Sector Reform and Development in Sierra Leone". Working Paper 11/0560.

Jordan, B., and Miller, T. 2009. *Fundamentals of Investment: Valuation and Measurement,* seventh edition. McMillan.

Jordan, B. D., and Miller, T. W. 2007. *Fundamentals of Investment, Valuation and Management,* eleventh edition.

Jorgenson, D. W., and Hall, R. 1971. "Application of the Theory of Optimum Capital Accumulation". In G. From (ed.), *Tax Incentives and Capital Spending,* Washington, DC: Brookings Institute.

Kahuthu, C. 1999. "Private Sector Development in Kenya: Prospect and Challenges". Working Paper, Nairobi, UNDP.

Kamps. 2005. "The Dynamic Effects of Public Capital: VAR Evidence for 22 OECD Countries". *International Tax and Public Finance Journal,* 12/4, 533–58.

Kandil, M., and Marsy, H. 2009. "Determinant of Inflation in Gulf Corporate Council (GCC)". IMF Working Paper WP/09/82.

Karumba, M. M. 2009. "The Impact of Institutional Factors and Liberalization Policies on Private Investment in Kenya (1965–2007)". Unpublished manuscript.

Keynes, J. M. 1936. *The General Theory of Employment, Interest and Money*. New York: Oxford University Press.

Khan, and Gill, A. R. 2009. "Crowing-out Effect of Public Borrowing. A Case of Pakistan". Paper presented at the eighth National Research Conference on Management and Computer Sciences, Islamabad, Pakistan.

Kimani, R. N. 2005. "The Relationship between Budget Deficit Financing and Private Investment in Kenya 1970–2003". Unpublished manuscript.

Kiptui, M. 2005. "Impact of Fiscal Policy on Private Investment in Kenya Institute of Policy Analysis and Research". Discussion Paper No. 066/2005, Nairobi: IPAR.

Kosimbei, G. 2009. "Budget Deficits and Macroeconomic Performance in Kenya (1963–2007): An Empirical Analysis". Unpublished manuscript.

Kumhof, M., et al. 2005. "Government Debt a Key Role in Financial Intermediation". IMF Working Paper WP/05/57.

Lamikanra, B. 2015. "How the Finance Sector Can Drive Africa's Economic Growth". KPMG Nigeria Working Paper.

Leonard, E. B., and Joel, S. 2013. *Taxes in America: What Everybody Wants to Know.* Oxford University Press.

Lesotho, P. 2006. "An Investigation of the Determinants of Private Investment: The Case of Botswana". Unpublished manuscript.

Linnemann, L. 2006. "The Transmission of Fiscal Policy Shocks in a New Keynesian Framework". *Scottish Journal of Political Economy.*

M'Amanja, D., and Morrisey, O. 2005. "Fiscal Policy and Economic Growth in Kenya". Centre for Research in Economic Development and International Trade Credit Research Paper No. 05/06, Nottingham, United Kingdom: University of Nottingham.

Maingi, J. N. 2010. "The Impact of Government Expenditure on Economic Growth (1963–2008)". Unpublished manuscript.

Martin, W. E., and Rawthrone, R. 2004. "Will Stability Last". CESifo Working Paper No. 1324, CESifo GmbH.

McCoy, D. 1997. "How Useful Is Structural VAR Analysis for Irish Economy?" Paper resented at an international seminar of the Central Bank of Ireland, Auckland, New Zealand: Central Bank of Ireland.

Megginson, W. L., Scott, B. S., and Lucy, M. 2008. *Introduction to Corporate Finance.* London: South-Western Cengage Learning EMEA.

Kalecki, M. 1984. *Capitalism: Business Cycles and Full Employment,* vol. 1. Oxford University Press.

Mills, S., and Zhoa, X. 2013. "Impact of Macroeconomic Factors on Economic Growth in Ghana: A Cointegration Analysis". *International Journal of Academic Research in Accounting, Finance and Management Sciences,* 3/1, 35–45.

Minsky, M. 1975. "Theory of Financial Crisis in the Global Context". *Journal of Economic Issues,* 36/2 (June 2002).

Morisset, J., and Pirnia, N. 2000. "How Tax Policy and Incentive Affect Foreign Direct Investment: A Review". Policy Paper 2509.

Moshi, H., and Kilindo, A. 1999. "The Impact of Growth Policy on Macroeconomic Variables: The Case of Private Investment in Tanzania". African Economic Research Consortium Research Paper No 89, Nairobi: AERC.

Motlaleng, R. 2011. *Effectiveness of Fiscal Spending in the Presence of Persistent Budget Deficit in Namibia: Crowding-Out or Crowding-In.* University of Botswana.

Munnell, A. H. 1990. "Infrastructure, Investment and Economic Growth". *Economic Perspective,* 64 (Fall 1992), 189–98.

Mwakoloba, A. B. S. 2009. "Economic Reforms in Eastern African Countries: The Impact on Governance Revenue and Public Investment". Unpublished manuscript.

National Revenue Authority. 2013. News Bulletin.

Njuru, G. 2012. "Effect of Fiscal Policy on Private Investment in Kenya". Paper presented at an international seminar of the Central Bank of Ireland, Republic of Ireland.

Nlovo, G. 2013. "Financial Sector Development and Economic Growth: Evidence from Zimbabwe". *International Journal of Economics and Financial Issues; Mersin 3.2.*

Oshikoya, W. T., and Tarawallie, S. A. 2010. "Sustainability of Fiscal Policy, The West African Monetary Zone (WAMZ) Experience". *Journal of Monetary Economic Integration.*

Perotti, R. 2004. *Estimating the Effects of Fiscal Policy in OECD Countries.* https://www.google.com.sl/search?q=Perotti.+%282004%29&oq=Perotti.

Philips, A. W. 1958. "The Relationship between Unemployment and the Rate of Change of Money Wages Rates in the United Kingdom 1861–1957". *Economica,* vol. 24, 283–99 *Representation, Estimation and Testing". Econometrica.* Vol 55, 251–276.

Phillips and Pughi. 2005. *A Handbook for Students and their Supervisors,* fourth edition). Open University Press.

Piana, V. 2001. "Investment". http://economicwebinstitute.org/glossary.invest.html.

Pickson, R. B. 2016. *The Nexus between Government Investment Expenditure and Private Investment in Ghana.* Research Gate. http://www.researchgate.net/publication/304673452.

Pigato, M., Farah, C., Itakura, K., Jun, K., Martin, W., Murrell, K., and Srinivasan, T. G. 2001. "South Asia's Integration into the World Economy". Working Paper, World Bank, Washington, DC.

Pindyck, R. S. 1991. "Irreversibility, Uncertainty and Investment". *Journal of Economic Literature,* 29/3, 1110–48.

Riley, G. 2012. *Economic Growth—The Role of Human and Social Capital, Competition and Innovation.* http://www.tutor2u.net/economics/revision-notes/a2-macro-economic-growth-capital.html.

Roemer, P. M. 1989. "Capital Accumulation in the 4 Theory on Long Run Growth". In R. Barro (ed.), *Modern Macroeconomics,* Ambridge, MA: Harvard University Press.

Rose, P. S. 1983. *Money and Capital Markets.* Plana, TX: Business Publications.

Roubini, E., and Sala-i-Martin. 1992. "Financial Repression and Economic Growth". *Journal of Development Economics,* 39/1, 5–30.

Samuel, A., Mills, E., and Zhoa, X. 2013. "Impact of Macroeconomic Factors on Economic Growth in Ghana". *International Journal of Academic Research in Accounting, Finance and Management Sciences.*

Schmidt-Hebbel, K. 1995. "Fiscal Adjustment and Growth in and Out of Africa". Africa Economic Research Consortium Special Paper No. 19, Nairobi: Regal Press.

Schroeman. 2000. "Foreign Direct Investment Determinant in Sub-Saharan Africa: A Co-integration Analysis". *Economic Bulletin,* 6/4, 1–19.

Seruvata and Jayaraman, T. K. 2001. "Determinant of Private Investment in Fiji". Working Paper, Reserve Bank of Fiji, Economic Department, 2001–2002, Suva, Fiji: Reserve Bank of Fiji.

Shaw, E. S. 1973. *Financial Deepening in Economic Development.* New York: Oxford University Press.

Sherman Act. 1890. https://www.britannica.com/event/ Sherman-Antitrust-Act.

Sierra Leone Government. 2013. *Agenda for Prosperity.*

Sierra Leone Government. 2008. "Poverty Reduction Strategy Paper 2".

Sierra Leone Ministry of Finance and Economic Development. 2012. *Economic Bulletin 2012.*

Sierra Leone State House. 2013. *Government Economic Updates.* http://www.state.gov/r/pa/ei/bgn/5475.htm.

Sierra Leone World Guide. 2009. *Sierra Leone Geography.* https://www.worldtravelguide.net/guides/africa/ sierra-leone/weather-climate-geography.

Sierra Rutile. 2000. *Hand Book*. Sierra Rutile Company. http://www.google.com.sl/url?sa=t&rct=j&q=&esrc=s&source=web&cd=1&ved=0ahUKEwiys_D2ZrVAhXEqxoKHXzEDz4QFgggMAA&url=http%3A%2F%2Fwww.sierra-rutile.com%2Fmedia%2F64098%2FSierra-Rutile-Corporate-Presentation_june13presentation_website.pdf&usg=AFQjCNH2Tm7smDiFg03ygaAzuB4cr42A9g.

Sims, C. 1980. "Macroeconomics and Reality". *Econometrica*, 48, 1–48.

Spense, D. A. 2006. *Investment and Capital Accumulation. Economic and Economic Change.* Open University Course DD202 team, 293.

Stiglitz, J. E. 1989. *The Economic Role of the State*. Oxford University Press.

Stock, J. H., and Watson, M. W. 2001. "Vector Auto Regressions". *Journal of Economic Perspectives*, 15, 101115.

Stotsky, A., and Mariam, J. G. 1997. "Tax Effort in Africa". Working Paper, International Monetary Fund.

Tatom, J. A. 1991. "Public Capital and Private Sector Performance". Working Paper, Federal Reserve Bank of St. Louis Review, 3–15.

Tobin, J. 1969. "A General Equilibrium Approach to Monetary Theory". *Journal of Money, Credit and Banking*, 1, 15–29.

Tondl, G. 2004. *Macroeconomic Effects of Fiscal Policies in Acceding Countries.* Mimeo: Vienna University of Economics.

Trading Economics. n.d. https://tradingeconomics.com/sierra-leone/gdp-growth-annual.

Trotman, D. T. 1997. *Economics of the Public Sector.* London: Macmillan.

United Kingdom National Budget Office. 2005. *National Budget Review.* https://www.google.com.sl/#q=United+Kingdom, +National+Budget+Office.+(2005)&spf=1500573518469.

United Kingdom National Statistics. 2004. *National Accounts Review.* Blue Book of the National Statistics.

United Nations. 1993. "Explaining and Forecasting Regional Inflows of Foreign Direct Investment". Working Paper, UNDP New York.

United Nations. 2001. Conference on Trade and Development, Geneva.

United States Office of Federal Budget. 2000. *Federal Budget.* http://federal budget.insidegov.com/l/103/2000.

Wawrie, N. H. W. 2003. "Trends in Kenya Tax Ratios and Effort Indices, and Their Implications for Future Tax Reforms in Illieva". *EV, Egerton Journal,* 4, 256–79.

Weeks, J. 2009. *The Global Financial Crisis and Countercyclical Fiscal Policy, Key Presentation at the 2009 African Caucus on the Global Crisis and Africa: Responses, Lesson Learnt and the Way Forward, Freetown, Sierra Leone* ... See CDPR Discussion Paper 26/09. Vol. 24, 21–24 Western Cape, Cape Town, South Africa.

World Bank. 2007. *African Data Base* (CD-ROM). Washington, DC: World Bank.

World Bank. 2012. *Introduction to the Basic Concept of Investment.* www.vangurl.co.uk/documents/partal/literature/investmentfundamental.

World Bank. 2014. *Decentralization, Accountability and Local Services in Sierra Leone: Situation Analysis, Key Challenges and Opportunities for Reforms.* World Bank.

World Bank Group. 2015. "Global Economic Prospects Divergences and Risks". https://www.google.com.sl/#q=world+bank+group+2015+economic+outlook&spf=1500656152111.

Zuber-Skeritt, O., and Knight, N. H. 1986. "Problems Definitions and Thesis Writing". Springerling Article.

APPENDICES

ANSWER

APPENDIX 1

Private Investment of Sierra Leone, 1980–2015

	YEAR	PINV	Ch. In PI
1	1980	136021.5419	
2	1981	168001.3081	24%
3	1982	105248.2844	-37%
4	1983	113733.4072	8%
5	1984	121813.9275	7%
6	1985	88639.27186	-27%
7	1986	74628.61869	-16%
8	1987	85012.00423	14%
9	1988	47158.62524	-45%
10	1989	68867.52453	46%
11	1990	99823.46121	45%
12	1991	78970.24297	-21%
13	1992	36729.48889	-53%
14	1993	24802.17792	-32%
15	1994	46910.79926	89%
16	1995	18193.40606	-61%
17	1996	74725.5675	311%
18	1997	-35294.11994	-147%
19	1998	3530.318795	-110%
20	1999	-18577.88614	-626%
21	2000	-37331.54803	101%
22	2001	52997.15917	-242%
23	2002	67502.46151	27%
24	2003	65279.03805	-3%
25	2004	60622.88002	-7%
26	2005	67888.62167	12%
27	2006	97323.55002	43%
28	2007	93680.68703	-4%
29	2008	93812.88776	0%
30	2009	101350.2764	8%
31	2010	358551.7141	254%
32	2011	322144.0714	-10%
33	2012	228545.034	-29%
34	2013	137586.1405	-40%
35	2014	214644.8104	56%
36	2015	213729.1784	0%

APPENDIX 2

Private Investment to Gross Domestic Products of Sierra Leone, 1980–2015

	YEAR	PINV	GDP	PI % GDP	Ch. In GDP	Ch. In PI
1	1980	136021.5419	1426717.36	10%		
2	1981	168001.3081	1435747.18	12%	1%	24%
3	1982	105248.2844	1472217.65	7%	3%	-37%
4	1983	113733.4072	1409700.61	8%	-4%	8%
5	1984	121813.9275	1432700.55	9%	2%	7%
6	1985	88639.27186	1321507.06	7%	-8%	-27%
7	1986	74628.61869	1299211.26	6%	-2%	-16%
8	1987	85012.00423	1350463.6	6%	4%	14%
9	1988	47158.62524	1218727.64	4%	-10%	-45%
10	1989	68867.52453	1200042.93	6%	-2%	46%
11	1990	99823.46121	1223524.49	8%	2%	45%
12	1991	78970.24297	1247638.85	6%	2%	-21%
13	1992	36729.48889	1014725.34	4%	-19%	-53%
14	1993	24802.17792	1037996.28	2%	2%	-32%
15	1994	46910.79926	1027102.12	5%	-1%	89%
16	1995	18193.40606	950045.997	2%	-8%	-61%
17	1996	74725.5675	967907.081	8%	2%	311%
18	1997	-35294.11994	908552.761	-4%	-6%	-147%
19	1998	3530.318795	916424.56	0%	1%	-110%
20	1999	-18577.88614	882288.14	-2%	-4%	-626%
21	2000	-37331.54803	915051.8	-4%	4%	101%
22	2001	52997.15917	817601.923	6%	-11%	-242%
23	2002	67502.46151	985226.657	7%	21%	27%
24	2003	65279.03805	1025366.74	6%	4%	-3%
25	2004	60622.88002	1041261.96	6%	2%	-7%
26	2005	67888.62167	1043357.97	7%	0%	12%
27	2006	97323.55002	1064906.21	9%	2%	43%
28	2007	93680.68703	1119152.14	8%	5%	-4%
29	2008	93812.88776	1151656.02	8%	3%	0%
30	2009	101350.2764	1161977.99	9%	1%	8%
31	2010	358551.7141	1196827.34	30%	3%	254%
32	2011	322144.0714	1222945.19	26%	2%	-10%
33	2012	228545.034	1378846.4	17%	13%	-29%
34	2013	137586.1405	1630572.57	8%	18%	-40%
35	2014	214644.8104	1668804.89	13%	2%	56%
36	2015	213729.1784	1217875.26	18%	-27%	0%

APPENDIX 3

Private Investment and Government Recurrent Expenditure of Sierra Leone, 1980–2015

	YEAR	PINV	GRExp	Chn. In PI	Chn in RE	PI % GREx
1	1980	136021.5419	140045.905			97%
2	1981	168001.3081	137559.054	24%	-2%	122%
3	1982	105248.2844	165189.986	-37%	20%	64%
4	1983	113733.4072	161804.472	8%	-2%	70%
5	1984	121813.9275	144012.415	7%	-11%	85%
6	1985	88639.27186	168358.544	-27%	17%	53%
7	1986	74628.61869	170450.716	-16%	1%	44%
8	1987	85012.00423	130833.355	14%	-23%	65%
9	1988	47158.62524	75326.981	-45%	-42%	63%
10	1989	68867.52453	80975.08	46%	7%	85%
11	1990	99823.46121	71499.5377	45%	-12%	140%
12	1991	78970.24297	91069.8818	-21%	27%	87%
13	1992	36729.48889	64619.5412	-53%	-29%	57%
14	1993	24802.17792	78543.4813	-32%	22%	32%
15	1994	46910.79926	82338.2693	89%	5%	57%
16	1995	18193.40606	62636.3923	-61%	-24%	29%
17	1996	74725.5675	82188.6004	311%	31%	91%
18	1997	-35294.11994	55958.9797	-147%	-32%	-63%
19	1998	3530.318795	54528.4616	-110%	-3%	6%
20	1999	-18577.88614	63166.8814	-626%	16%	-29%
21	2000	-37331.54803	92887.7581	101%	47%	-40%
22	2001	52997.15917	97466.28	-242%	5%	54%
23	2002	67502.46151	124925.545	27%	28%	54%
24	2003	65279.03805	116105.36	-3%	-7%	56%
25	2004	60622.88002	102093.495	-7%	-12%	59%
26	2005	67888.62167	101849.024	12%	0%	67%
27	2006	97323.55002	107544.342	43%	6%	90%
28	2007	93680.68703	92560.3791	-4%	-14%	101%
29	2008	93812.88776	101859.2	0%	10%	92%
30	2009	101350.2764	110417.317	8%	8%	92%
31	2010	358551.7141	111929.673	254%	1%	320%
32	2011	322144.0714	111633.655	-10%	0%	289%
33	2012	228545.034	126022.541	-29%	13%	181%
34	2013	137586.1405	131222.609	-40%	4%	105%
35	2014	214644.8104	110901.288	56%	-15%	194%
36	2015	213729.1784	101161.689	0%	-9%	211%

APPENDIX 4

Private Investments and Government Development Expenditure of Sierra Leone, 1980–2015

	YEAR	PINV	GDExp	Ch. In PI	Ch. In GDEx	PI % GDEx
1	1980	136021.5419	97046.4404			140%
2	1981	168001.3081	91042.6684	24%	-6%	185%
3	1982	105248.2844	91510.1605	-37%	1%	115%
4	1983	113733.4072	78321.8989	8%	-14%	145%
5	1984	121813.9275	60049.6689	7%	-23%	203%
6	1985	88639.27186	49702.1213	-27%	-17%	178%
7	1986	74628.61869	50770.202	-16%	2%	147%
8	1987	85012.00423	46360.3026	14%	-9%	183%
9	1988	47158.62524	46697.0813	-45%	1%	101%
10	1989	68867.52453	71170.3837	46%	52%	97%
11	1990	99823.46121	124560.899	45%	75%	80%
12	1991	78970.24297	116348.348	-21%	-7%	68%
13	1992	36729.48889	74204.3481	-53%	-36%	49%
14	1993	24802.17792	75712.2252	-32%	2%	33%
15	1994	46910.79926	89199.2627	89%	18%	53%
16	1995	18193.40606	52000.1634	-61%	-42%	35%
17	1996	74725.5675	130665.817	311%	151%	57%
18	1997	-35294.11994	26434.6966	-147%	-80%	-134%
19	1998	3530.318795	50862.9095	-110%	92%	7%
20	1999	-18577.88614	2587.49577	-626%	-95%	-718%
21	2000	-37331.54803	61839.7727	101%	2290%	-60%
22	2001	52997.15917	80349.5476	-242%	30%	66%
23	2002	67502.46151	97226.6004	27%	21%	69%
24	2003	65279.03805	104675.623	-3%	8%	62%
25	2004	60622.88002	100602.263	-7%	-4%	60%
26	2005	67888.62167	118809.072	12%	18%	57%
27	2006	97323.55002	110524.194	43%	-7%	88%
28	2007	93680.68703	107889.324	-4%	-2%	87%
29	2008	93812.88776	106736.923	0%	-1%	88%
30	2009	101350.2764	112178.898	8%	5%	90%
31	2010	358551.7141	372720.832	254%	232%	96%
32	2011	322144.0714	518061.882	-10%	39%	62%
33	2012	228545.034	364230.153	-29%	-30%	63%
34	2013	137586.1405	301516.833	-40%	-17%	46%
35	2014	214644.8104	313875.566	56%	4%	68%
36	2015	213729.1784	318287.205	0%	1%	67%

APPENDIX 5

Private Investment and Total Government Spending of Sierra Leone, 1980–2015

	YEAR	PINV	SPE	Ch. In SPE	PI %SPE	Ch. In PI
1	1980	136021.5419	237092.345		57%	
2	1981	168001.3081	228601.722	-4%	73%	24%
3	1982	105248.2844	256700.146	12%	41%	-37%
4	1983	113733.4072	240126.371	-6%	47%	8%
5	1984	121813.9275	204062.084	-15%	60%	7%
6	1985	88639.27186	218060.665	7%	41%	-27%
7	1986	74628.61869	221220.918	1%	34%	-16%
8	1987	85012.00423	177193.658	-20%	48%	14%
9	1988	47158.62524	122024.062	-31%	39%	-45%
10	1989	68867.52453	152145.464	25%	45%	46%
11	1990	99823.46121	196060.437	29%	51%	45%
12	1991	78970.24297	207418.23	6%	38%	-21%
13	1992	36729.48889	138823.889	-33%	26%	-53%
14	1993	24802.17792	154255.707	11%	16%	-32%
15	1994	46910.79926	171537.532	11%	27%	89%
16	1995	18193.40606	114636.556	-33%	16%	-61%
17	1996	74725.5675	212854.418	86%	35%	311%
18	1997	-35294.11994	82393.6763	-61%	-43%	-147%
19	1998	3530.318795	105391.371	28%	3%	-110%
20	1999	-18577.88614	65754.3771	-38%	-28%	-626%
21	2000	-37331.54803	154727.531	135%	-24%	101%
22	2001	52997.15917	177815.828	15%	30%	-242%
23	2002	67502.46151	222152.146	25%	30%	27%
24	2003	65279.03805	220780.984	-1%	30%	-3%
25	2004	60622.88002	202695.758	-8%	30%	-7%
26	2005	67888.62167	220658.095	9%	31%	12%
27	2006	97323.55002	218068.536	-1%	45%	43%
28	2007	93680.68703	200449.703	-8%	47%	-4%
29	2008	93812.88776	208596.123	4%	45%	0%
30	2009	101350.2764	222596.215	7%	46%	8%
31	2010	358551.7141	484650.505	118%	74%	254%
32	2011	322144.0714	629695.538	30%	51%	-10%
33	2012	228545.034	490252.694	-22%	47%	-29%
34	2013	137586.1405	432739.443	-12%	32%	-40%
35	2014	214644.8104	424776.854	-2%	51%	56%
36	2015	213729.1784	419448.895	-1%	51%	0%

APPENDIX 6

Private Investment and Private Consumption
of Sierra Leone, 1980–2015

	YEAR	PINV	PCON	Ch. In PI	PI. % PCON	Ch. In PCON
1	1980	136021.5419	1604555.93		8%	
2	1981	168001.3081	1525706.64	24%	11%	-5%
3	1982	105248.2844	1468093.47	-37%	7%	-4%
4	1983	113733.4072	1330581.16	8%	9%	-9%
5	1984	121813.9275	1271233.12	7%	10%	-4%
6	1985	88639.27186	1151789.37	-27%	8%	-9%
7	1986	74628.61869	1091841.6	-16%	7%	-5%
8	1987	85012.00423	1190438.14	14%	7%	9%
9	1988	47158.62524	993381.03	-45%	5%	-17%
10	1989	68867.52453	1051367.67	46%	7%	6%
11	1990	99823.46121	870769.557	45%	11%	-17%
12	1991	78970.24297	864382.665	-21%	9%	-1%
13	1992	36729.48889	782210.736	-53%	5%	-10%
14	1993	24802.17792	834577.211	-32%	3%	7%
15	1994	46910.79926	686341.213	89%	7%	-18%
16	1995	18193.40606	851877.664	-61%	2%	24%
17	1996	74725.5675	898768.144	311%	8%	6%
18	1997	-35294.11994	745411.386	-147%	-5%	-17%
19	1998	3530.318795	715544.152	-110%	0%	-4%
20	1999	-18577.88614	660072.541	-626%	-3%	-8%
21	2000	-37331.54803	653025.128	101%	-6%	-1%
22	2001	52997.15917	808998.772	-242%	7%	24%
23	2002	67502.46151	950326.244	27%	7%	17%
24	2003	65279.03805	968923.56	-3%	7%	2%
25	2004	60622.88002	961195.097	-7%	6%	-1%
26	2005	67888.62167	941419.222	12%	7%	-2%
27	2006	97323.55002	921272.143	43%	11%	-2%
28	2007	93680.68703	982175.835	-4%	10%	7%
29	2008	93812.88776	1040924.6	0%	9%	6%
30	2009	101350.2764	1118462.26	8%	9%	7%
31	2010	358551.7141	966111.506	254%	37%	-14%
32	2011	322144.0714	1175090.22	-10%	27%	22%
33	2012	228545.034	1284070.56	-29%	18%	9%
34	2013	137586.1405	1320200.06	-40%	10%	3%
35	2014	214644.8104	1100666.93	56%	20%	-17%
36	2015	213729.1784	1000396.63	0%	21%	-9%

APPENDIX 7

Private Investment and Total Tax Revenue of Sierra Leone, 1980–2015

	YEAR	PINV	TREV	Ch. In PI	PI. % TREV	Ch. In. TREV
1	1980	136021.5419	234349.594		172%	
2	1981	168001.3081	245105.887	24%	146%	5%
3	1982	105248.2844	166536.306	-37%	158%	-32%
4	1983	113733.4072	116992.903	8%	103%	-30%
5	1984	121813.9275	120148.436	7%	99%	3%
6	1985	88639.27186	86647.2628	-27%	98%	-28%
7	1986	74628.61869	80624.2283	-16%	108%	-7%
8	1987	85012.00423	75960.5746	14%	89%	-6%
9	1988	47158.62524	82882.718	-45%	176%	9%
10	1989	68867.52453	79416.5051	46%	115%	-4%
11	1990	99823.46121	68380.3767	45%	69%	-14%
12	1991	78970.24297	96956.6758	-21%	123%	42%
13	1992	36729.48889	105730.25	-53%	288%	9%
14	1993	24802.17792	129169.931	-32%	521%	22%
15	1994	46910.79926	129417.442	89%	276%	0%
16	1995	18193.40606	89201.5779	-61%	490%	-31%
17	1996	74725.5675	97491.5254	311%	130%	9%
18	1997	-35294.11994	49356.4592	-147%	-140%	-49%
19	1998	3530.318795	67293.1063	-110%	1906%	36%
20	1999	-18577.88614	62695.0692	-626%	-337%	-7%
21	2000	-37331.54803	104673.195	101%	-280%	67%
22	2001	52997.15917	79193.143	-242%	149%	-24%
23	2002	67502.46151	90424.6736	27%	134%	14%
24	2003	65279.03805	91600.3115	-3%	140%	1%
25	2004	60622.88002	96141.5401	-7%	159%	5%
26	2005	67888.62167	92268.9117	12%	136%	-4%
27	2006	97323.55002	94530.5685	43%	97%	2%
28	2007	93680.68703	93246.0884	-4%	100%	-1%
29	2008	93812.88776	103293.592	0%	110%	11%
30	2009	101350.2764	104756.463	8%	103%	1%
31	2010	358551.7141	117633.321	254%	33%	12%
32	2011	322144.0714	141731.758	-10%	44%	20%
33	2012	228545.034	159028.288	-29%	70%	12%
34	2013	137586.1405	177361.875	-40%	129%	12%
35	2014	214644.8104	168819.776	56%	79%	-5%
36	2015	213729.1784	131155.555	0%	61%	-22%

APPENDIX 8

Private Investment and Indirect Taxes
of Sierra Leone, 1980–2015

	YEAR	PINV	IDT	Ch. In PI	IDT. % PI	Ch. In IDT
1	1980	136021.5419	146577.803		108%	
2	1981	168001.3081	151513.251	24%	90%	3%
3	1982	105248.2844	109426.11	-37%	104%	-28%
4	1983	113733.4072	74583.5943	8%	66%	-32%
5	1984	121813.9275	65673.2741	7%	54%	-12%
6	1985	88639.27186	55256.4388	-27%	62%	-16%
7	1986	74628.61869	36279.4351	-16%	49%	-34%
8	1987	85012.00423	46299.1591	14%	54%	28%
9	1988	47158.62524	52206.1486	-45%	111%	13%
10	1989	68867.52453	78297.5209	46%	114%	50%
11	1990	99823.46121	49700.1203	45%	50%	-37%
12	1991	78970.24297	71203.2669	-21%	90%	43%
13	1992	36729.48889	78520.1292	-53%	214%	10%
14	1993	24802.17792	96797.2827	-32%	390%	23%
15	1994	46910.79926	98188.4648	89%	209%	1%
16	1995	18193.40606	67694.0565	-61%	372%	-31%
17	1996	74725.5675	58433.3666	311%	78%	-14%
18	1997	-35294.11994	69697.6309	-147%	-197%	19%
19	1998	3530.318795	51068.1168	-110%	1447%	-27%
20	1999	-18577.88614	42982.743	-626%	-231%	-16%
21	2000	-37331.54803	71961.2829	101%	-193%	67%
22	2001	52997.15917	52948.6369	-242%	100%	-26%
23	2002	67502.46151	61292.7582	27%	91%	16%
24	2003	65279.03805	62033.3751	-3%	95%	1%
25	2004	60622.88002	60707.9447	-7%	100%	-2%
26	2005	67888.62167	58072.2201	12%	86%	-4%
27	2006	97323.55002	62597.2976	43%	64%	8%
28	2007	93680.68703	57467.3122	-4%	61%	-8%
29	2008	93812.88776	60909.4745	0%	65%	6%
30	2009	101350.2764	62166.2094	8%	61%	2%
31	2010	358551.7141	76917.9731	254%	21%	24%
32	2011	322144.0714	89840.7375	-10%	28%	17%
33	2012	228545.034	59950.8498	-29%	26%	-33%
34	2013	137586.1405	60242.5028	-40%	44%	0%
35	2014	214644.8104	64011.6534	56%	30%	6%
36	2015	213729.1784	69460.3414	0%	32%	9%

APPENDIX 9

Private Investment and Personal Income
Taxes of Sierra Leone, 1980–2015

	YEAR	PINV	PIT	Ch. In PI	PIT. % PI	Ch. In PIT
1	1980	136021.5419	20683.9777		15%	
2	1981	168001.3081	26737.6325	24%	16%	29%
3	1982	105248.2844	19310.49	-37%	18%	-28%
4	1983	113733.4072	13161.8108	8%	12%	-32%
5	1984	121813.9275	11589.4013	7%	10%	-12%
6	1985	88639.27186	8163.74199	-27%	9%	-30%
7	1986	74628.61869	5360.02598	-16%	7%	-34%
8	1987	85012.00423	6840.36824	14%	8%	28%
9	1988	47158.62524	7713.08351	-45%	16%	13%
10	1989	68867.52453	8096.20962	46%	12%	5%
11	1990	99823.46121	5074.09605	45%	5%	-37%
12	1991	78970.24297	7269.44348	-21%	9%	43%
13	1992	36729.48889	8016.45298	-53%	22%	10%
14	1993	24802.17792	10195.6529	-32%	41%	27%
15	1994	46910.79926	10342.186	89%	22%	1%
16	1995	18193.40606	7130.21153	-61%	39%	-31%
17	1996	74725.5675	6154.78354	311%	8%	-14%
18	1997	-35294.11994	11256.0773	-147%	-32%	83%
19	1998	3530.318795	8247.43488	-110%	234%	-27%
20	1999	-18577.88614	6941.65746	-626%	-37%	-16%
21	2000	-37331.54803	11621.6542	101%	-31%	67%
22	2001	52997.15917	12851.6109	-242%	24%	11%
23	2002	67502.46151	12360.1419	27%	18%	-4%
24	2003	65279.03805	11007.2977	-3%	17%	-11%
25	2004	60622.88002	12468.3456	-7%	21%	13%
26	2005	67888.62167	12230.2319	12%	18%	-2%
27	2006	97323.55002	13561.251	43%	14%	11%
28	2007	93680.68703	15160.0885	-4%	16%	12%
29	2008	93812.88776	15132.7887	0%	16%	0%
30	2009	101350.2764	17496.4646	8%	17%	16%
31	2010	358551.7141	17929.0815	254%	5%	2%
32	2011	322144.0714	31613.1317	-10%	10%	76%
33	2012	228545.034	13710.5411	-29%	6%	-57%
34	2013	137586.1405	14716.1649	-40%	11%	7%
35	2014	214644.8104	15855.9349	56%	7%	8%
36	2015	213729.1784	19466.311	0%	9%	23%

APPENDIX 10

Private Investment and Corporation Tax of Sierra Leone, 1980–2015

	YEAR	PINV	CIT	Ch. In PI	CIT. % PI	Ch. In CIT
1	1980	136021.5419	31821.5041		23%	
2	1981	168001.3081	33952.5492	24%	20%	7%
3	1982	105248.2844	24521.2571	-37%	23%	-28%
4	1983	113733.4072	16713.4105	8%	15%	-32%
5	1984	121813.9275	14716.7001	7%	12%	-12%
6	1985	88639.27186	12245.613	-27%	14%	-17%
7	1986	74628.61869	8040.03898	-16%	11%	-34%
8	1987	85012.00423	10260.5524	14%	12%	28%
9	1988	47158.62524	11569.6253	-45%	25%	13%
10	1989	68867.52453	16192.4192	46%	24%	40%
11	1990	99823.46121	10278.2971	45%	10%	-37%
12	1991	78970.24297	14725.2829	-21%	19%	43%
13	1992	36729.48889	16238.456	-53%	44%	10%
14	1993	24802.17792	15846.2557	-32%	64%	-2%
15	1994	46910.79926	16074	89%	34%	1%
16	1995	18193.40606	11081.895	-61%	61%	-31%
17	1996	74725.5675	9565.86839	311%	13%	-14%
18	1997	-35294.11994	9184.95911	-147%	-26%	-4%
19	1998	3530.318795	6729.90686	-110%	191%	-27%
20	1999	-18577.88614	5664.39249	-626%	-30%	-16%
21	2000	-37331.54803	9483.26984	101%	-25%	67%
22	2001	52997.15917	7637.52877	-242%	14%	-19%
23	2002	67502.46151	11005.6058	27%	16%	44%
24	2003	65279.03805	12287.216	-3%	19%	12%
25	2004	60622.88002	12812.2999	-7%	21%	4%
26	2005	67888.62167	15223.6453	12%	22%	19%
27	2006	97323.55002	13651.0606	43%	14%	-10%
28	2007	93680.68703	15424.5086	-4%	16%	13%
29	2008	93812.88776	16835.2274	0%	18%	9%
30	2009	101350.2764	18180.6839	8%	18%	8%
31	2010	358551.7141	15826.288	254%	4%	-13%
32	2011	322144.0714	13644.9842	-10%	4%	-14%
33	2012	228545.034	14789.3484	-29%	6%	8%
34	2013	137586.1405	15863.0252	-40%	12%	7%
35	2014	214644.8104	15983.5537	56%	7%	1%
36	2015	213729.1784	15982.3384	0%	7%	0%

APPENDIX 11

Changes in Private Sector Credit Ratios
of Sierra Leone, 1980–2015

	YEAR	PS/CR	Ch. In PS/CR
1	1980	7.8675897880	
2	1981	7.6806995821	-0.023754442
3	1982	7.0881894671	-0.077142728
4	1983	7.0513298865	-0.00520014
5	1984	4.0773035354	-0.421768149
6	1985	3.0978234549	-0.240227413
7	1986	5.4148073022	0.747939281
8	1987	2.7438590856	-0.493267455
9	1988	3.4964291531	0.274274314
10	1989	4.8277364928	0.380761995
11	1990	3.2474843982	-0.327327744
12	1991	3.5226360136	0.084727617
13	1992	3.0533759729	-0.133212753
14	1993	3.4316905072	0.12390041
15	1994	3.1281570017	-0.08845014
16	1995	2.6764264436	-0.144407892
17	1996	2.5068221188	-0.063369694
18	1997	3.2454112637	0.294631653
19	1998	2.7245156247	-0.160502197
20	1999	2.0718272999	-0.239561234
21	2000	2.1080336091	0.017475544
22	2001	1.6202621949	-0.231386925
23	2002	2.0238130261	0.24906514
24	2003	2.8927132023	0.429338168
25	2004	3.5156471452	0.215345905
26	2005	3.3922275625	-0.035105794
27	2006	3.3837484285	-0.002499577
28	2007	4.3270441852	0.278772426
29	2008	5.5748215143	0.288367134
30	2009	8.1053034363	0.453912635
31	2010	7.7084486139	-0.048962365
32	2011	7.5562053513	-0.019750182
33	2012	6.1358201925	-0.187975987
34	2013	4.7323620494	-0.228731954
35	2014	4.7211507420	-0.002369072
36	2015	4.8628241303	0.030008232

APPENDIX 12

Change in Private Sector Credit versus Change in Real Interest Rates of Sierra Leone, 1980–2015

	Year	RIR	Ch. In PS/CR	Ch. In RIR
1	1980	11		
2	1981	15	-0.023754442	0.36363636
3	1982	15	-0.077142728	0
4	1983	17.25	-0.00520014	0.15
5	1984	18	-0.421768149	0.04347826
6	1985	17	-0.240227413	-0.0555556
7	1986	17.19	0.747939281	0.01117647
8	1987	28.54	-0.493267455	0.6602676
9	1988	28	0.274274314	-0.0189208
10	1989	29.67	0.380761995	0.05964286
11	1990	52.5	-0.327327744	0.76946411
12	1991	56.25	0.084727617	0.07142857
13	1992	62.83	-0.133212753	0.11697778
14	1993	50.46	0.12390041	-0.1968805
15	1994	27.33	-0.08845014	-0.4583829
16	1995	28.83	-0.144407892	0.05488474
17	1996	32.12	-0.063369694	0.11411724
18	1997	23.87	0.294631653	-0.2568493
19	1998	23.83	-0.160502197	-0.0016757
20	1999	26.83	-0.239561234	0.12589173
21	2000	26.25	0.017475544	-0.0216176
22	2001	24.27	-0.231386925	-0.0754286
23	2002	22.17	0.24906514	-0.0865266
24	2003	20	0.429338168	-0.09788
25	2004	22.08	0.215345905	0.104
26	2005	24.58	-0.035105794	0.11322464
27	2006	24	-0.002499577	-0.0235964
28	2007	25	0.278772426	0.04166667
29	2008	24.5	0.288367134	-0.02
30	2009	22.17	0.453912635	-0.095102
31	2010	21.25	-0.048962365	-0.0414975
32	2011	21	-0.019750182	-0.0117647
33	2012	21	-0.187975987	0
34	2013	20.56	-0.228731954	-0.0209524
35	2014	19.41	-0.002369072	-0.0559339
36	2015	20.644	0.030008232	0.06357548

APPENDIX 13

Change in Private Sector Credit versus Money
Supply of Sierra Leone, 1980–2015

	Year	MS	PS/CR	Ch. in MS
1	1980	260790000		
2	1981	267630000	-0.023754442	0.026228
3	1982	419640000	-0.077142728	0.56798565
4	1983	552370000	-0.00520014	0.31629492
5	1984	708750000	-0.421768149	0.28310734
6	1985	1212650000	-0.240227413	0.71097002
7	1986	2284640000	0.747939281	0.8840061
8	1987	3747220000	-0.493267455	0.64017963
9	1988	5878500000	0.274274314	0.56876298
10	1989	10240240000	0.380761995	0.7419818
11	1990	17817890000	-0.327327744	0.73998754
12	1991	31397490000	0.084727617	0.76213289
13	1992	41833500000	-0.133212753	0.33238358
14	1993	51004450000	0.12390041	0.21922502
15	1994	55497100000	-0.08845014	0.08808349
16	1995	66382700000	-0.144407892	0.19614719
17	1996	86063812000	-0.063369694	0.29647953
18	1997	1.26633E+11	0.294631653	0.47138614
19	1998	1.40899E+11	-0.160502197	0.11265844
20	1999	1.94159E+11	-0.239561234	0.37799681
21	2000	2.17605E+11	0.017475544	0.12075809
22	2001	2.85539E+11	-0.231386925	0.31218959
23	2002	3.68599E+11	0.24906514	0.29088608
24	2003	4.49774E+11	0.429338168	0.2202259
25	2004	5.40409E+11	0.215345905	0.20151332
26	2005	7.08722E+11	-0.035105794	0.31145425
27	2006	8.62235E+11	-0.002499577	0.21660548
28	2007	1.00976E+12	0.278772426	0.17109332
29	2008	1.27774E+12	0.288367134	0.26538996
30	2009	1.71893E+12	0.453912635	0.34529625
31	2010	2.13414E+12	-0.048962365	0.24154893
32	2011	2.76644E+12	-0.019750182	0.29627992
33	2012	3.37464E+12	-0.187975987	0.2198469
34	2013	3.37464E+12	-0.228731954	0
35	2014	4.56867E+12	-0.002369072	0.35382612
36	2015	5.10133E+12	0.030008232	0.11658793

APPENDIX 14

Change in Private Sector Credit versus Inflation of Sierra Leone, 1980–2015

		INF	Ch. In INF	Ch. In PS/CR
1	1980	6.008734537		
2	1981	8.698312242	0.447611338	-0.0237544
3	1982	18.50162731	1.127036464	-0.0771427
4	1983	19.43895601	0.05066196	-0.0052001
5	1984	39.7672586	1.045750738	-0.4217681
6	1985	68.88971428	0.732322436	-0.2402274
7	1986	78.5037958	0.139557576	0.74793928
8	1987	165.67664	1.110428398	-0.4932675
9	1988	64.28824806	-0.611965525	0.27427431
10	1989	61.49127685	-0.043506726	0.38076199
11	1990	70.59154925	0.1479929	-0.3273277
12	1991	128.7616683	0.824038	0.08472762
13	1992	82.02357923	-0.362981388	-0.1332128
14	1993	26.73632213	-0.674041021	0.12390041
15	1994	25.06204274	-0.062621904	-0.0884501
16	1995	33.59798913	0.340592604	-0.1444079
17	1996	29.58048516	-0.119575727	-0.0633697
18	1997	2.252769698	-0.923842706	0.29463165
19	1998	23.77512107	9.55372908	-0.1605022
20	1999	17.19385039	-0.27681334	-0.2395612
21	2000	3.281143083	-0.809167638	0.01747554
22	2001	73.55826648	21.41848789	-0.2313869
23	2002	3.935269946	-0.946501323	0.24906514
24	2003	13.19430676	2.352833971	0.42933817
25	2004	12.82500384	-0.027989566	0.21534591
26	2005	16.61545327	0.295551523	-0.0351058
27	2006	12.48606454	-0.248526998	-0.0024996
28	2007	6.796157752	-0.455700575	0.27877243
29	2008	9.992262197	0.470281085	0.28836713
30	2009	7.783062926	-0.221091003	0.45391263
31	2010	17.17691878	1.206961314	-0.0489624
32	2011	17.66914902	0.028656492	-0.0197502
33	2012	11.70133328	-0.337753433	. -0.187976
34	2013	6.692763746	-0.428034089	-0.228732
35	2014	0.190579757	-0.971524506	-0.0023691
36	2015	10.60991701	54.67179416	0.03000823

APPENDIX 15

The Private Sector Ratio and Other Fiscal Policy Variables Compared of Sierra Leone, 1980–2015

	Ch. In PS/CR	Ch. In RIR	Ch. APA	Ch. MS	Ch. PSCF	Ch. In INF
1980						
1981	0.000505051	0.000505051	2.09090909	0.026228	0.3725391	0.447611338
1982	0.000504796	0.000504796	0.67973856	0.567985652	-0.2413905	1.127036464
1983	0.000504541	0.000504541	0.21011673	0.316294919	0.319576	0.05066196
1984	0.000504286	0.000504286	3.79421222	0.283107337	0.5332306	1.045750738
1985	0.000504032	0.000504032	0.33735748	0.710970018	0.2615845	0.732322436
1986	0.000503778	0.000503778	0.49197593	0.884006102	0.5475745	0.139557576
1987	0.000503525	0.000503525	6.16134521	0.640179634	2.1220982	1.110428398
1988	0.000503271	0.000503271	0.62849084	0.568762976	-0.0616328	-0.611965525
1989	0.000503018	0.000503018	0.17192677	0.741981798	1.4125211	-0.043506726
1990	0.000502765	0.000502765	0.65691097	0.739987539	1.5065147	0.1479929
1991	0.000502513	0.000502513	1.25055663	0.76213289	0.8164943	0.824038
1992	0.00050226	0.00050226	-0.209504	0.332383576	-0.1569851	-0.362981388
1993	0.000502008	0.000502008	-0.3714447	0.219225023	-0.1518793	-0.674041021
1994	0.000501756	0.000501756	3.44816853	0.088083491	1.3439583	-0.062621904
1995	0.000501505	0.000501505	-1.2236612	0.196147186	-0.4846538	0.340592604
1996	0.000501253	0.000501253	1.12228152	0.296479535	4.3156516	-0.119575727
1997	0.000501002	0.000501002	0.12872096	0.471386138	-1.4842695	-0.923842706
1998	0.000500751	0.000500751	-0.4448591	0.112658443	-1.1249344	9.55372908
1999	0.000500501	0.000500501	2.51424702	0.377996807	-7.2790123	-0.27681334
2000	0.00050025	0.00050025	2.829058	0.120758085	1.1342116	-0.809167638
2001	0.0005	0.0005	-0.2831302	0.312189593	-3.5606655	21.41848789
2002	0.00049975	0.00049975	0.31547498	0.290886076	0.2821299	-0.946501323
2003	0.0004995	0.0004995	-0.1206781	0.220225903	0.1504905	2.352833971
2004	0.000499251	0.000499251	-0.5915712	0.201513319	0.0979956	-0.027989566
2005	0.000499002	0.000499002	-0.7757964	0.311454254	0.3597615	0.295551523
2006	0.000498753	0.000498753	-7.0219953	0.216605478	0.6672489	-0.248526998
2007	0.000498504	0.000498504	-0.808179	0.171093317	0.0569835	-0.455700575
2008	0.000498256	0.000498256	-10.725774	0.265389963	0.1281847	0.470281085
2009	0.000498008	0.000498008	0.61330344	0.345296253	0.1908635	-0.221091003
2010	0.00049776	0.00049776	-4.7229616	0.241548934	3.2399042	1.206961314
2011	0.000497512	0.000497512	-1.5823478	0.296279922	0.7039107	0.028656492
2012	0.000497265	0.000497265	-1.0812502	0.219846904	-0.2361321	-0.337753433
2013	0.000497018	0.000497018	1.60677215	0	-0.2802509	-0.428034089
2014	0.000496771	0.000496771	-19.994602	0.353826122	-0.0733133	-0.971524506
2015	0.000496524	0.000496524	-0.4758688	0.116587928	0.098279	54.67179416

Printed in the United States
By Bookmasters